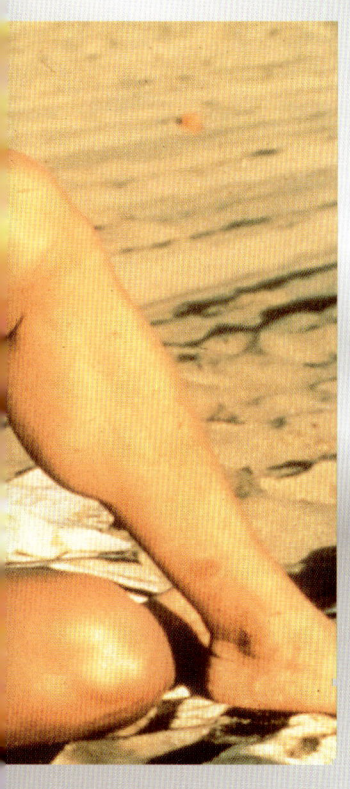

ARNOLD
Schwarzenegger

by Bob McCabe

AN ORION PAPERBACK

This is a Carlton Book

First published in Great Britain in 1994 by Orion Books Ltd,
Orion House, 5 Upper St Martin's Lane, London WC2H 9EA

Text and design copyright © 1994 Carlton Books Limited
CD Guide format copyright © 1994 Carlton Books Limited

All rights reserved. No part of this publication may be reproduced, stored in a retrieval system, or transmitted, in any form or by any means, electronic, mechanical, photocopying, or otherwise, without the prior permission of the copyright owner.

A CIP catalogue record for this book is available from the British Library.

ISBN 1-85797-329-1

Edited, designed and typeset by Haldane Mason
Printed in Italy

THE AUTHOR
Bob McCabe is Film Editor of *Vox* magazine. He has also freelanced for a number of mainstream magazines, including *Premiere* and *Empire*, and works as a film reviewer on BBC Radio, GLR and Sky TV.

Photographs reproduced by kind permission of **London Features International**; **Pictorial Press**/Conde-SF,/Jacobs,/Natkin-SF,/Vinnie Zuffante; **Rex Features**/ Globe Photos,/Joffett,/MC Laughlin,/Charles Sykes,/Trippett.
Front cover picture: Pictorial Press

Contents

Introduction 6

Hercules and the Early Years 8

Mr Olympia 22

From Barbarian to Terminator 42

Total Stardom 72

Last Action Hero 106

Chronology 114

Filmography 117

Index 119

Introduction

Arnold Schwarzenegger is an extraordinary person. At 6'4" with the physique of a world-class bodybuilder, international success as a movie star, one of the highest salaries in the world, a happy marriage and acceptance into the most élite of social circles, he seems to have it all. What makes him extraordinary is that every aspect of his life and success has been gained through determination, hard work and an astute business sense. Arnold is the epitome of the American dream—the totally self-made man in every sense, with the intelligence and vision to build and expand on each new success rather than to rest on his laurels.

At each stage of his life, Arnold has set himself goals, and in each case has not simply achieved the goal but has become the best in his field several times over. Beginning in the gymnasiums of Graz in Austria he rose to become a world-champion bodybuilder, and then used the fame and money he earned to go into business, swiftly becoming a millionaire. Finally, having firmly established himself in the public eye, he moved into the lucrative world of the movies.

From an unspectacular beginning with *Hercules Goes Bananas*, in which his inimitable voice was dubbed, he built a championship movie career with the same precision with which he once built his body. Comic-book capers like the *Conan* movies were followed by spectacular action adventures, ground-breaking science-fiction thrillers with top-flight directors, and, finally, an unusually successful transition to comedy. Never one to do things by halves, Arnold starred in Hollywood's most expensive film of its time, the record-breaking *Terminator 2: Judgment Day*, and in just about its biggest flop of recent years, *Last Action Hero*.

What Arnold Schwarzenegger has achieved in his career is both remarkable and unrivalled, and it might seem that he has gone as high as he can go. But to date he has always managed to improve on each peak in his career—so what remains to be seen is what he will do next.

INTRODUCTION

CHAPTER 1

Hercules and the Early Years

> It's hard to imagine anyone being inspired by *Hercules and the Captive Women* or *Hercules Against the Moon Men*.

But to one young boy sitting in a provincial theatre in a small Austrian town, these low-budget, badly made and badly dubbed "B" movies were a revelation. The character was a god, the performer was a movie star, and the body was perfection. To Arnold Schwarzenegger, these were ideals he would strive to realize for himself.

Arnold Schwarzenegger (the surname literally translates as "black ploughman") was born on July 30, 1947 in the rural town of Thal in Austria. His father, Gustav, was the local police chief, and a talented musician who played in, and sometimes led, the police band, Gendarmerie Musik. On October 20, 1945, at the age of 38, Gustav had married Aurelia Jadrny, an attractive young widow 15 years his junior. In July of the following year their first son, Meinhard, was born, followed just over a year later by Arnold.

Arnold attended the local Hans Grass School, where he played soccer, something

Kirk Douglas was one of the many movie heroes that Arnold watched and admired as a young boy in the local cinemas in Graz.

HERCULES AND THE EARLY YEARS

> **"I was like this great car with nowhere to go. I had the drive but I needed to get focused and figure out what the end should look like."**
>
> **Arnold Schwarzenegger**

his father hoped he would pursue, although later it would become clear that team sports were not for Arnold.

Escape to the movies
Stuck in a remote peasant town and overshadowed by his elder brother, the teenage Arnold was unsure of his destiny. "I was like this great car with nowhere to go," he once said. "I had the drive but I needed to get focused and figure out what the end should look like." He found at least a glimpse of that end product in the cinemas of Graz. Here Arnold spent innumerable hours revelling in the escapism of Hollywood and the strong physical images of the likes of John Wayne and Kirk Douglas.

But it was a character called Hercules that really left a mark. The *Hercules* movies were a low-budget series, originating in Italy and poorly dubbed into English, which found a degree of worldwide success in the late Fifties

American movie stars like John Wayne were some of Arnold's earliest role models.

ARNOLD SCHWARZENEGGER

HERCULES AND THE EARLY YEARS

> "It is one thing to idolize heroes. It is quite another to visualize yourself in their place. When I saw great people, I said to myself, 'I can be there.'"
> **Arnold Schwarzenegger**

and early Sixties. The character of Hercules was played by a succession of bodybuilders, including Steve Reeves, Alan Steel and Reg Park, Arnold's personal favourite, who would later become his friend. Watching these low-grade movies in his early teens, Arnold could not have known that he would one day play the character of Hercules himself on screen, but instinctively he recognized that these were people he wanted to emulate.

Steve Reeves in the part of Hercules, the role that would launch Arnold's own movie career.

Building the perfect body

Demonstrating the same drive he would show throughout his career, at the age of 15 Arnold took control of his destiny and began to work towards the dream of becoming a bodybuilder. "As a kid I always idolized the winning athletes," he said. "It is one thing to idolize heroes. It is quite another to visualize yourself in their place. When I saw great people, I said to myself, 'I can be there.'"

Opposite page: **Arnold's bodybuilding success drew attention to a sport that had often been ridiculed in the past.**

ARNOLD SCHWARZENEGGER

The triumphant Mr Universe.

HERCULES AND THE EARLY YEARS

Within a year, getting there began to look possible when he met Kurt Marnul, a former Mr Austria. Impressed by the young Schwarzenegger—already 6' 2"—Kurt invited Arnold to train at Marnul's Athletic Union in Graz. Arnold's brother Meinhard accompanied him at first, but had no real serious interest in bodybuilding. Arnold, however, became totally dedicated to the regimen of the sport, training all hours, seven days a week, forsaking girls and his regular church attendance in favour of barbells and the bench press.

The extraordinary success that Arnold achieved in his field combined with his winning personality made him a highly marketable author.

Military man
On October 1, 1965, four months after his eighteenth birthday, Arnold began his National Service in the Austrian army. Still finding every opportunity to work out, Arnold became a tank driver, obviously something he enjoyed, as today he drives a "Humvee", a US military vehicle of tank-like proportions.

Less than a month after he was conscripted into the army, Arnold went AWOL to attend his first major bodybuilding contest, the Junior Mr Europe, held on October 30, 1965. He won, and later described his reaction as: "I thought I was King Kong."

In his book, *Arnold: The Education of a Bodybuilder*, published in 1977, he wrote of the army punishment he received for his unauthorized absence—a week in the brig. But quietly his division were proud of him and encouraged his training, seeing his achievements as a source of national pride.

Aurelia Schwarzenegger poses with her little boy.

Mr Germany meets Mr Universe

In March 1966 Arnold won the Mr Germany contest, his second major title, and by August of that year he was working as a trainer at a prestigious gym in Munich and building himself up for his first major international contest.

In September 1966 he attended the National Amateur Body Building Association (NABBA) Mr Universe contest in London. For Arnold, the Universe contest was all-important. Sean Connery had once been a competitor, and Mickey Hargitay, whom Arnold would later play in *The Jayne Mansfield Story,* was a former winner of the title. Arnold came second, beaten by American Chet Yorton, but Arnold's charm as well as his impressive physique captivated the audience, and announced that a new force had emerged on the bodybuilding scene.

After the show, Arnold renewed an acquaintance with English bodybuilding enthusiast and gym owner Wag Bennett. Through Wag, Arnold finally got to meet his boyhood hero, one-time Hercules Reg Park, and they posed together at one of Wag's London shows.

The youngest Universe

Arnold returned to London the following September to claim at last the title of Mr Universe. At 6' 2", 235 lbs, with 22-inch biceps, a 31-inch

HERCULES AND THE EARLY YEARS

> "I hope that you are not going to go away and write that I am, how do you say, all brain and no brawns."
>
> **Arnold to *Daily Mirror* reporter**

The greatest body in the world—it's official.

waist and a 57-inch chest, Arnold, at the age of 20, became the youngest Mr Universe ever.

Arnold's latest triumph brought him to the attention of American publisher Joe Weider, who was keen to take him to America— both to train and to write manuals for his publishing company—in the hope of making him the biggest bodybuilding star in the world. However, Arnold was already set on retaining his Mr Universe title, and would not take up Weider's offer for another year.

Meet the press

In March 1968 Arnold gave his first major English-speaking interview to the *Daily Mirror* newspaper in London. "Please understand that I am like an ordinary man only bigger and stronger," he told the reporter. "I hope that you are not going to go away and write that I am, how do you say, all brain and no brawns."

ARNOLD SCHWARZENEGGER

Mirror, mirror on the wall, who is the greatest of them all?

Unfortunately this was not the case. The piece instead took a derisory tone, playing on Arnold's limited English and expanded physique to picture him as something of a musclebound fool. It was an example that he learned from, realizing that an image can be successfully created and protected only if one is aware of, and able to use fully, the media that presents it. Interestingly, the *Daily Mirror* piece also claimed that at this point Arnold had already been offered several film roles, including Hercules, Tarzan and Samson, although it would be nearly two years before he made his movie début.

Mr Universe hits America
Now posing to the heroic strains of the theme from *Exodus*, Arnold stormed the 1968 Mr Universe contest, claiming his second crown in the event on September 21, 1968. Days later he was making the most important journey of his life, on a plane from London bound for America, and the beginnings of a business relationship with Joe Weider that would make him both a rich man and a virtual god in the world of bodybuilding.

Just one day after his arrival in America, however, Arnold was defeated in the International Federation of Body Builders (IFBB) Mr Universe contest (the American equivalent of the European title he had just successfully defended) by Mr America winner Frank Zane. Discouraged by such an inauspicious American début, Arnold later told US magazine *Rolling Stone*: "I had no money. I had only one gym bag with me, because I did not plan to move here at that point. I was kind of like a helpless kid in a way."

But, as he was to do repeatedly throughout his career, Arnold took this defeat and turned it into a drive for victory. He would stay in America,

Building the perfect body—Arnold's dedication brought him fresh triumphs in 1968.

ARNOLD SCHWARZENEGGER

train, adapt and rebuild himself as a success in the image of the American dream—a child from a poor background who, if he couldn't quite grow up to be President, could at least become friends with him.

Arnold realizes his childhood ambition to become a god in *Hercules in New York* (1970).

The Austrian Oak

Arnold set to work immediately. Nicknamed the "Austrian Oak" by Joe Weider, he relocated to Santa Monica, with its nearby Muscle Beach, a mecca for bodybuilders. At Weider's expense, Arnold's close friend

HERCULES AND THE EARLY YEARS

and fellow bodybuilder Franco Columbu, whom Arnold first met at the Junior Mr Europe contest, flew over to work with him. They shared an apartment near the gym where Arnold trained compulsively. Columbu recalled, "He never said, 'I am going to compete.' Always, 'I am going to win.'"

Part of Arnold's Americanization involved Weider's astute head for business; under his influence, Arnold invested his money in real estate, which made him a millionaire while he was still in his twenties. In return Weider was using Arnold, under the stage name "Arnold Strong", as an image and personality to market a range of mail-order bodybuilding aids and training manuals.

In September 1969, Arnold entered the IFBB Mr Olympia contest, but was once again relegated to position of runner-up, this time by Sergio Oliva, who would remain Arnold's most potent rival over the next few

Arnold proves how difficult it is to get a cab in Times Square: *Hercules in New York* (1970).

> "He never said, 'I am going to compete.' Always, 'I am going to win.'"
> **Franco Columbu**

ARNOLD SCHWARZENEGGER

Opposite page: Arnold's first billing, as Arnold Strong, shows how far he had to go to reach the sophistication of his later films, such as The Terminator (1984).

years. By means of compensation, Arnold travelled back to London to defend with ease his NABBA title of Mr Universe, which only reinforced his determination to conquer America's bodybuilding championships.

Hercules Goes Bananas

On his return to the US, Arnold was greeted with his first movie role, won for him by mentor Weider. *Hercules in New York* (often known by the title *Hercules Goes Bananas*) must have offered Arnold a great deal of personal satisfaction, as he found himself in the place of his long-time hero Reg Park. However, this low-budget Italian production (the press

Arnold's early casual but nondescript appearance bears little resemblance to the larger-than-life movie star image that was soon to replace it.

HERCULES AND THE EARLY YEARS

release for which read "The action never stops. He is chased by beautiful girls, fight promoters, grizzly bears, gangsters and an angry Zeus hurling thunderbolts, all culminating in an uproarious chariot race through Times Square") was an unlikely début for the man who would go on to become one of the world's biggest movie stars. "Every so often," he has said, "I get twenty phone calls from people laughing, saying, we have seen this most hideous thing on television."

The movie did not represent what Arnold wanted from his career, and, if anything, submerged the powerful personality and image that would come to be such a dominant screen force, as he performed under the Weider moniker of Arnold Strong, and suffered the further indignity of having his voice dubbed due to his heavy accent and relatively poor English.

Hercules In New York may have marked the beginning of Arnold Schwarzenegger's film career, may even have offered something of a small personal triumph as he emulated his childhood hero, but it also marked the last time the powerful Schwarzenegger personality would be buried behind a façade. For now, however, the Austrian Oak was more concerned with his first career, and the long-coveted Mr Olympia title.

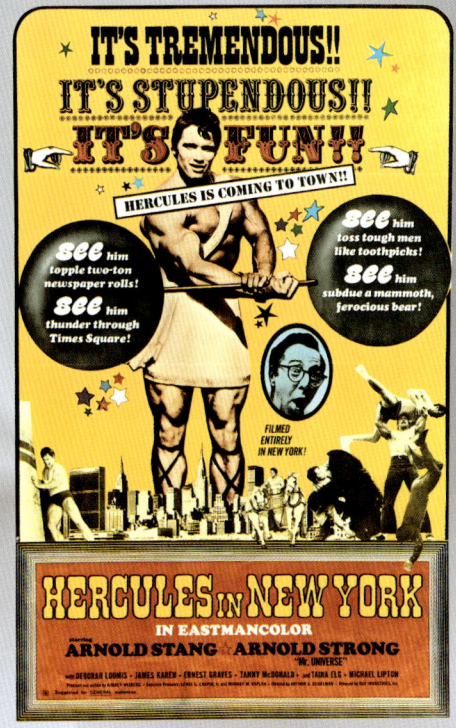

CHAPTER 2

Mr Olympia

> **Not surprisingly, movie offers did not come flooding in on the strength of *Hercules in New York*.**

Arnold spent most of 1970 marketing his and Weider's highly profitable series of bodybuilding booklets, and, of course, in training.

During this time Arnold continued to absorb himself into his adopted country, to which he had grown more than attached. "America represented a place where there was much success, progress, and no limit to one's vision," he explained. "I realized I had much more the American spirit." That spirit was making him a rich man, thanks to his real estate and publishing deals, but still one thing eluded him. This would be the year to change all that.

The triple

On September 18, Arnold set in motion an historic chain of events when he won the NABBA Mr Universe title in Britain for the fourth consecutive year, beating, among others, Reg Park, who was attempting a short-lived comeback. Literally collecting his trophy and jumping straight on a plane, Arnold headed for Columbus, Ohio to compete in the Pro Mr World contest the following day. The prospect of US television coverage was too good an opportunity to pass up, and Arnold beat rival Sergio Oliva to pick up the title.

MR OLYMPIA

"America represented a place where there was much success, progress, and no limit to one's vision... I realized I had much more the American spirit."

Arnold Schwarzenegger

Two weeks later, on October 3, Arnold finally won the coveted Mr Olympia crown. Now at the peak of his powers, Arnold had won all three major bodybuilding titles—Mr Universe, Mr World and Mr Olympia—in one year. At the age of 23, he had proved himself unbeatable in his chosen arena.

One event marred Arnold's enjoyment of success. On May 20 the following year, his brother Meinhard died in a car accident, one month before he was due to be married. Arnold did not attend the funeral.

The Triple Crown winner: Mr World, Mr Olympia and Mr Universe.

Opposite page: The Austrian Oak adopts a new homeland.

ARNOLD SCHWARZENEGGER

An early publicity shot.

> "It was clear that Arnold was a star. His presence was just incredible."
>
> **George Butler**

An Olympian in Paris

In 1971, the IFBB passed a new regulation excluding any bodybuilder competing in the NABBA Mr Universe from entering their own Mr Olympia title. Arnold, who had originally planned to defend both his titles, now found himself forced to choose one, and opted for the more prestigious Olympia. In the competition in Paris that year, he kept his title.

Arnold had achieved everything it was possible to achieve in the bodybuilding world. His success had taken a long-derided sport and given it credibility, his masculinity helping to dispel the image of homosexuality long attached to bodybuilding. "The biggest cliché going around was that the sport attracted a lot of homosexuals," he said. "Yes, the sport attracts homosexuals, but it also attracts old ladies, young girls and all kinds of men." He had spent years achieving his dream of becoming, effectively, the world champion, but now it had been achieved, Arnold

MR OLYMPIA

was anxious to move beyond the world of bodybuilding, to become a household name away from the sport, and to become a different kind of star.

Pumping Iron

At the Mr America competition in Brooklyn in 1972, Arnold met someone who was to help him achieve all this. George Butler was a photographer, working with Charles Gaines, a writer who was planning a book on the sport to be titled *Pumping Iron*. Butler was instantly captivated by Arnold. "It was clear that Arnold was a star. His presence was just incredible."

Ordinarily a book on bodybuilding would not be expected to be a big seller, but the possibility of a tie-in movie, and more importantly, his potential starring role in it, led Arnold to agree to work with Butler and Gaines, a move that was to prove to be a significant step towards movie stardom.

Two months after Arnold successfully defended his Mr Olympia title, his father, Gustav, died of a heart attack. Again Arnold did not attend the funeral. In one of *Pumping Iron*'s many telling moments,

Arnold claims not to be obsessive about his sport, and finds other ways of working out.

ARNOLD SCHWARZENEGGER

Arnold explains for the benefit of the camera that he wasn't able to attend his father's funeral because he was busy training. In fact, he didn't hear the news until a week after the funeral. He was later to say: "My father saw the progress—that I was developing in my sport and was smart in business—but he never saw the full circle."

Movie heavy

In 1973 Arnold was back before the cameras, working with established director Robert Altman, who had recently had major success with a string of idiosyncratic movies, such as M*A*S*H and Brewster McCloud. The project was a modern updating of Raymond Chandler's classic novel The Long Goodbye, with Elliot Gould as private eye Philip Marlowe. Sadly, though a prestigious movie, this was not exactly a pivotal film role for Arnold, who was only briefly on screen with no dialogue as a "heavy", giving Gould a hard time.

By the time of the 1974 Mr Olympia contest, Arnold was facing competition from a newcomer, 22-year-old Lou Ferrigno. Ferrigno would go on to appear in Pumping Iron with Arnold, and would ironically also one day play Hercules (in a 1983 movie), but would find his greatest success as the

MR OLYMPIA

green half of the TV series *The Incredible Hulk*.

The *Pumping Iron* book had just been published and was selling surprisingly well, so public awareness of bodybuilding was running high. Arnold didn't miss the opportunity to maintain his profile, and defeated Ferrigno to keep his title.

Filling the small screen

Thanks to the success of the book and his many bodybuilding titles, Arnold was now an active promoter of the sport, racking up numerous television appearances and gradually becoming accustomed to finding himself in front of the camera. He used it to promote his image of Arnold the self-made man, the immigrant come to America to fulfil his dream—but also Arnold the personality, who didn't take things too seriously: a man rather than a bodybuilding machine. "I think I made the sport more acceptable when I promoted bodybuilding in the mid Seventies," he said. "If you want to make people join a certain activity, you have to make it pleasant-sounding. I talked about the diet, but I said I eat cake and ice cream as well."

You can't teach an old dog new tricks, but you can teach him bad habits.

It became clear that these self-promoting appearances were having the right effect when comedienne Lucille Ball, after seeing Arnold on *The Merv Griffin Show*, invited him to appear on her 1974 TV special *Happy*

ARNOLD SCHWARZENEGGER

Opposite page: **Famous for their chest measurements: Dolly Parton and Arnold Schwarzenegger.**

Frequent chat-show appearances gave Arnold an on-screen confidence that he has continued to use to his advantage.

Anniversary and Goodbye, a high-profile network show, co-starring Art Carney, which saw Arnold playing it for laughs as a musclebound masseuse.

Staying hungry

Thanks to the television exposure, Arnold was becoming increasingly comfortable in front of the camera, and was learning how to use it for his own ends, so the time seemed right to give acting another try. Determined not to make any more mistakes along the lines of *Hercules in New York*, he began to search for a quality picture.

His friend *Pumping Iron* author Charles Gaines came to his assistance. Another of Gaines's novels, *Stay Hungry*, was being filmed by director Bob Rafelson, who had previously scored a major hit with Jack Nicholson in *Five Easy Pieces*. The film was already set to star Jeff Bridges and Sally Field, and Gaines suggested casting Arnold as bodybuilder Joe Santo. Arnold won the role, although the part was noticeably reduced, with Rafelson insisting he take several weeks of intensive acting lessons before filming began on location in Birmingham, Alabama in April 1975. Although trade paper *Variety* described the movie as "a lurching and poorly defined film concept," Arnold came out of it feeling that he had learned a good deal about acting: "I tapped a new well I had never tapped

MR OLYMPIA

before." It also marked another significant career move for Arnold: already firmly established in the world of sport, he could now appear under his real surname. Arnold Strong was no more.

Pumping up

With another role under his belt, Arnold—who was still taking acting lessons—was ready to give his best performance yet. In the film of *Pumping Iron* he would play maybe his finest role, that of himself, Arnold Schwarzenegger, the self-made man, the body made perfect, the strong, competitive but also wise-cracking and of course successful champion, a creation of personality as impressive as his biceps and pecs. In short, the living, breathing embodiment of the American dream in god-like proportions.

Arnold knew that *Pumping Iron* was make or break time for his career. While the other competitors thought flexing for the cameras was all that was required, Arnold knew a personality as large as that 57-inch chest was needed to bring the audience into this unique world. He cast himself as that guide, neatly stealing Butler and Gaines's film, though both were only too happy to go along for the ride.

ARNOLD SCHWARZENEGGER

The strongest man gets the dressing-room: Arnold with Jeff Bridges in *Stay Hungry* (1976).

Pumping Iron is a remarkable film in many respects, partly because it captures the world of a relatively unknown sport, and partly because it catches a star on the rise. Right from the start, Schwarzenegger displays the combination of outstanding physique and appealing personality that

MR OLYMPIA

How Muscle Beach got its name.

first marked him out from the crowd at the 1966 Mr Universe contest. Focusing on the run-up to the 1975 Mr Olympia contest, *Pumping Iron* concentrates on a small number of competitors, Lou Ferrigno and Franco Columbu included. While they strain and struggle, Arnold gracefully practises ballet, the gentle giant giving his all for his art. He is at all times focused and relaxed and has an unerring knack for saying the right thing at the right time, relating the peak of his physical perfection to sex. "It is as satisfying to me as coming is—you know, as having sex with a woman and coming. So can you believe how much I am in heaven? I am getting the feeling of coming in the gym. I'm coming day and night." If anyone knew how to make bench-pressing sound an attractive proposition, it was Arnold Schwarzenegger.

Between bouts of training, Arnold recounts for the camera the story of

ARNOLD SCHWARZENEGGER

> "Arnold Schwarzenegger was the first man smart enough to transcend bodybuilding's dim obsessional gloom...Devoted as he was to training, he was even more devoted to the idea of himself as a winner."
> **David Denby**

Pumping Iron allowed Arnold to do what he did best—flex his muscles and charm the audience at the same time.

MR OLYMPIA

his success, his love of America, his representation of the ideal. He coolly smokes dope as he undermines the audience's confidence in the other competitors until he is all they want to see. It is a masterful performance, and by the time it arrives at the 1975 Mr Olympia in Pretoria, the outcome is more than a foregone conclusion, it is almost a supreme vindication, almost a divine right that he should win. The message was clear—here was a winner, a patriot, seriously ambitious yet still hip enough to smoke, with a killer smile and a big cigar. How could he be ignored?

Critic David Denby summed up the success of *Pumping Iron*: "Arnold Schwarzenegger was the first man smart enough to transcend bodybuilding's

Overleaf: **Arnold offers 1988's Mr Universe, Alph Miller, a cigar.**

The self-made man relaxes by the pool.

ARNOLD SCHWARZENEGGER

dim obsessional gloom...Devoted as he was to training, he was even more devoted to the idea of himself as a winner."

Pumping Iron remains one of the most blatant, most unashamed, and most mesmeric calling cards ever dropped on Hollywood's doorstep. Here was a star, ripe for the taking, and all of Tinseltown would be fools to ignore it.

The retiring king

At least that was the plan. The release of *Pumping Iron* was, however, delayed, not opening until January 1977. Before it came out, Arnold, perhaps spurred on by the great photo opportunity a camera crew allowed, announced his retirement from bodybuilding. "I felt at the time that if I continued my career in bodybuilding, my immediate needs would be satisfied. However, if one's needs are satisfied, then you lose the hunger to do anything else. So, I cut the ties, and knew I would eventually make a push in a new direction, which I later decided should be acting."

For the majority of 1976 Arnold was forced to wait. Knowing the goods were in the can with *Pumping Iron*, he just had to sit tight until the can was opened. To

MR OLYMPIA

> "I felt at the time that if I continued my career in bodybuilding, my immediate needs would be satisfied. However, if one's needs are satisfied, then you lose the hunger to do anything else. So I cut the ties."
>
> **Arnold Schwarzenegger**

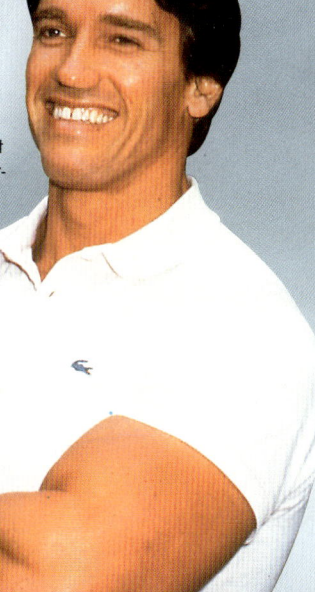

Arnold had good reason to smile, as he began to collect acting awards in place of his numerous bodybuilding titles.

keep busy, he became partners with Jim Lorimer to promote the Mr Olympia contest, held on September 18. He may not have been a competitor this time, but Arnold's presence pervaded the event, from the slant of the media coverage to the 4,000 fans in attendance, most of them attracted to the sport by the power of the Austrian Oak.

Golden Globe
Just days before *Pumping Iron* was due to open in January 1977, Arnold's new career received a boost when he won a Golden Globe Award for Best Newcomer, for his role in *Stay Hungry*, at a ceremony that also rewarded Sylvester Stallone (for *Rocky*), whom Arnold would one day

ARNOLD SCHWARZENEGGER

partner in the Planet Hollywood restaurant chain. But at this point, Stallone was on top, his movie a hit, with Oscars on the way, and Arnold had to be content with being the new muscleman on the block.

The New York opening of *Pumping Iron* on January 18 went some way to redress that balance. Sold heavily on the Schwarzenegger persona, the film was a cult hit, and nothing short of a cultural sensation in New York, where Arnold quickly became the man of the moment, photographed

Reagan-era icon Rambo made Sylvester Stallone the movies' biggest box-office draw.

MR OLYMPIA

> "No Tarzan roles for me...I want roles in films that express more emotion than swinging around the branches like monkeys."
>
> **Arnold Schwarzenegger**

From rivals to partners— Schwarzenegger and Stallone, two of the movies' biggest stars.

by Robert Mapplethorpe, and dining at Elaine's with Jackie Onassis. Although far removed from the sweat of the gym, he quickly took to this new café society.

Educated bodybuilder

Later in the year, Arnold published his first book, *Arnold: The Education of a Body Builder* (co-written with Douglas Kent Hall), which went on to become a top ten bestseller, and he travelled to Cannes to promote *Pumping Iron*. Cannes, probably the most public of film festivals, would later come to be defined by Arnold's regular visits— *Last Action Hero* saw 60-foot inflatable Arnolds straddling the harbour—but, even on this, his first trip, he was already a force to be reckoned with, as *Pumping Iron* proved to be a major festival hit.

At the festival, Arnold was already planning his acting future, and told UK critic Alexander Walker, "No Tarzan roles for me...I want roles in films that express more emotion than swinging around the

ARNOLD SCHWARZENEGGER

38

branches like monkeys." Whether Tarzan roles were all he was being offered, whether he was resting on the laurels of *Pumping Iron*, or whether he was rethinking his approach to his movie career, Arnold had a hard time finding a follow-up to his early movie success.

When he did return to movie-making, in the instantly forgettable comedy western *The Villain* (aka *Cactus Jack*), it was in a very minor role as the Handsome Stranger. Perhaps Arnold chose to do the movie for the opportunity of working with Kirk Douglas, one of his boyhood heroes. Whatever the reason, it was not a successful film, and one critic remarked that Arnold's horse was a good deal more expressive in its performance than its rider.

> "I knew instantly that Maria was the woman for my life, she was so full of life, so very beautiful. I loved her drive for success."
>
> **Arnold Schwarzenegger**

"I've just met a girl called Maria…"

If Arnold's career was on hold, then his personal life was anything but. On August 28 he attended the Robert F. Kennedy Tennis Tournament at Forest Hills, New York, and spent the following weekend as a guest of the Kennedy family in their home at Hyannis Port. Here he met Maria Shriver, a would-be TV journalist, niece of the late John F. Kennedy, and the woman Arnold would marry nine years later. He later said of the meeting, "I knew instantly that Maria was the woman for my life, she was so full of life, so very beautiful. I loved her drive for success."

Psycho bodybuilder

Unexpectedly, after his bravura turn in *Pumping Iron*, Arnold's film career was once more on hold. The thankless role in *The Villain* did nothing to help, aside from giving him the opportunity to travel with Maria to the

Opposite page: The Villain (aka Cactus Jack) gave Arnold the chance to work alongside his boyhood idol Kirk Douglas, pictured with co-star Ann-Margret.

ARNOLD SCHWARZENEGGER

The marriage of politics and Hollywood—Arnold steps out with JFK's niece Maria Shriver.

Cannes Film Festival to promote it. By the time he agreed to a guest spot on TV's popular *The Streets of San Francisco*, things seemed to be at an all-time low, as he was reduced to playing the role of a psychotic, woman-slaying bodybuilder.

He passed his time with business deals, furthering his education—he graduated from the University of Wisconsin with a business and international economics degree—and commentary duties for CBS's television coverage of bodybuilding.

MR OLYMPIA

Arnold Schwarzenegger was caught between two stools—though well known, he was the man who used to be a champion bodybuilder and who wasn't yet a movie star. It would take two mythical heroes to change all that. One was a barbarian; one was a god—Arnold would be both.

A smile and a big cigar—Arnold wallows in his success.

CHAPTER 3

From Barbarian to Terminator

> **Arnold has described the character of Conan as "God's gift to my career", and in many ways it was.**

Conan the Barbarian finally provided Arnold with the vehicle that would make him a mainstream movie star. He had previously tried out for the lead in producer Dino De Laurentiis's *Flash Gordon*, but lost the role to the blond, all-American Sam Jones. The producer was subsequently averse to casting Arnold as Conan, but maverick director John Milius insisted that Arnold the perfect body would make Arnold the perfect barbarian, and De Laurentiis was eventually persuaded. Filming on location in Spain was set for October 1980.

Prior to filming, Arnold co-starred in the TV movie *The Jayne Mansfield Story*, with Loni Anderson in the title role. Arnold played her husband, former Mr Universe Mickey Hargitay. Press reports at the time concentrated on the steamy relationship between Loni and Arnold during filming, but Arnold's screen performance recalled the best of his *Stay Hungry* work, showing the quiet, sensitive side of the muscle-heavy character.

The Comeback
Perhaps it was playing a former Mr Universe; perhaps it was being one. Either way, with *Conan the Barbarian* just a month away, Arnold resolved

to re-invent himself once more as the world's greatest bodybuilder, the only bodybuilder ever to stage a comeback five years after giving up the game.

The Mr Universe contest of September 1980 in Australia was for Arnold the ultimate challenge. Everyone knew he was attending—he had, after all, been contracted by CBS to act as a commentator—but no one knew he was competing. To the other contestants arriving in Sydney, the sudden appearance of Schwarzenegger, all ready to pump and flex, was a debilitating surprise.

Frank Zane, the reigning Mr Universe, and newcomer Mike Mentzer, bright young

Before his film career took over, Arnold was determined to prove himself one last time.

> **"After five years away from competition it was wonderful to use psychological warfare again."**
>
> **Arnold Schwarzenegger**

ARNOLD SCHWARZENEGGER

Both Arnold and Clint Eastwood (pictured here with Sondra Locke) benefited from the creative talents of John Milius: he not only worked on the scripts for the *Dirty Harry* films that Eastwood made famous, but also directed Arnold in *Conan the Barbarian*.

hope of the year, came thinking that it was a two-way competition, given Arnold's absence from the sport. Instead it was a walkover for Arnold, and the footage filmed there—later released as *The Comeback*—showed one thing clearly: Arnold was the crowd's favourite, a king come home to reign again.

Back to the movies

Soon after his triumph at the Mr Universe contest, Arnold headed for Spain and *Conan the Barbarian*, which was based on the popular series of books by Robert E. Howard, and the equally successful *Marvel* comic. Arnold knew this was a crucial move for his movie career, and may well

FROM BARBARIAN TO TERMINATOR

Behold my mighty sword! Arnold finds fame as Robert E. Howard's *Conan the Barbarian*.

Arnold with co-star Sandahl Bergman in a publicity shot for *Conan the Barbarian*.

have been using the Mr Universe comeback as a way to bolster his confidence, gearing himself up to play "this guy who's so in control with his sword, and he's so out of control".

Director Milius was an ideal choice for a movie about a lone barbarian. Long the outsider of Hollywood's so-called Movie Brats (Scorsese, Spielberg and Coppola included), he had co-written the original screenplay for *Apocalypse Now*, enshrined the character of Dirty Harry in his script for *Magnum Force*, and directed Sean Connery and Candice Bergen in *The Wind and the Lion*. He has described himself as "so far right, I'm probably an anarchist", and co-authored the *Conan* screenplay with the similarly iconoclastic director Oliver Stone (*Platoon*, *Born on the Fourth of July*).

Milius may have displayed some doubts about Arnold's acting abilities —"He's not a natural. He'll learn and he'll improve, but he's not an actor"—but one thing was clear. Though similarly attired to Hercules, the character of Conan the Barbarian was light years away from Arnold's acting début, allowing him to find, as he would often do, a character that meshed perfectly with the image of Schwarzenegger as icon—the once-again triumphant Mr Universe as a comic-book barbarian.

FROM BARBARIAN TO TERMINATOR

Conan hits

Conan the Barbarian grossed nearly $10 million (£6.7 million) in its first weekend of release in May 1982. It went on to take $41 million (£27.3 million) in the States, with a worldwide gross of over $100 million (£67 million), a phenomenal sum for its day. Reviews were mixed, with *Variety* commenting: "There is a real anticipation as Schwarzenegger is unveiled as the barbarian and sets off on the road to independence. But for whatever reasons, the actor has a minimum of dialogue and fails to convey much about the character through his actions." The character's sparsity of dialogue may have been a reflection of Milius's doubts about Arnold as an actor, something that clearly didn't bother its star, who said, "I have no ego for lines. I can say what I want on television when I do interviews."

Lack of lines aside, the movie was a hit, thanks in no small part to its star's capacity and willingness for self-promotion. One thing Arnold has never been afraid to do is promote his movies tirelessly, even taking a somewhat perverse pride in his ability to do 70-plus interviews in a single day. Applying the same principles he

> "He's not a natural. He'll learn and he'll improve, but he's not an actor."
>
> **John Milius**

ARNOLD SCHWARZENEGGER

applies to his successful and burgeoning business empire, Arnold sees each movie as an investment, something to be nurtured to ensure that the next one will be even bigger. Even on a movie as blatantly unsuccessful as *The Villain*, he was out there pressing the Cannes-tanned flesh. *Conan the Barbarian* gave him the backing of a major film and a major studio; consequently the self-made man turned movie star could be seen grinning from every magazine and publicizing himself on every available chat show.

Already accepted and welcomed by Hollywood, Arnold finally became an American citizen in 1983.

Arnie the American

Now a fully fledged Hollywood name, Arnold took the next step in his realization of the American dream on September 18, 1983. Dressed in red, white and blue he attended the ceremony that finally confirmed him as an American citizen. "In Europe people have a million reasons why you will never make it. Americans have such a wonderful history of growth. All the great things have happened to me since I came here." He kept his Austrian citizenship, but had now given himself up to his adopted country, his land of opportunity. Movies were one way of giving something back to that country; another was politics.

Conan the Republican

Since the mid Eighties, the name of Schwarzenegger has constantly been linked to Washington DC. The Kennedy

FROM BARBARIAN TO TERMINATOR

> "In Europe people have a million reasons why you will never make it. Americans have such a wonderful history of growth. All the great things have happened to me since I came here."
>
> **Arnold Schwarzenegger**

connection didn't hurt of course, and the press have often suggested Schwarzenegger for the roles of Governor of California and Senator. It has also been jokingly suggested the constitution be changed to allow a citizen not born in the US to run for President. Indeed, in one of a series of mutual cinematic digs, Sylvester Stallone made just that joke in *Demolition Man*, awakening in the future only to be directed to the President Schwarzenegger Library. And why not? After all, the image Arnold had spent the majority of his adult life carefully composing and nurturing was that of the archetypal American success story, the boy who works hard and grows up to have it all.

Arnold's public support of both Bush and Reagan earned him the nickname Conan the Republican.

ARNOLD SCHWARZENEGGER

Co-star Grace Jones *(far right)* proved to be more than a match for Arnold's barbarian skills in the inevitable sequel, *Conan the Destroyer* (1984).

Whatever the outcome of Schwarzenegger's alleged political aspirations, upon obtaining his citizenship he was quick to demonstrate publicly where his loyalties lay: firmly behind the politically conservative Ronald Reagan, whom Schwarzenegger publicly spoke out for when he attended the 1984 Republican convention in Dallas. The themes of Reagan's politics would run throughout the majority of Arnold's cinematic work—the American military world policing of *Predator*, the politically correct Glasnost-inspired *Red Heat*, the back-to-basics and love and support for the family in *Twins* and *Kindergarten Cop*. Perhaps, though, what Reagan represented best to Arnold was the ability to have it all. After all, here was a man who used to be a movie star, and he was now the leader of the strongest nation on Earth.

Destroying Conan

With his politics on the back burner, where they have largely remained throughout his career, Arnold was soon back in front of the cameras, filming the sequel to his first major hit, suitably titled *Conan the Destroyer*. The more sombre approach of Milius's superior original was replaced now by the lighter vision of director Richard Fleischer (*Dr Doolittle*, *Tora! Tora! Tora!*). Statuesque model/singer/famous-for-being-famous celebrity Grace Jones was also on hand, to provide Arnie with a suitably sizeable sidekick.

The barbarian and "the Bitch"—Arnold with superstar Joan Collins at the launch of her book *Past Imperfection*.

ARNOLD SCHWARZENEGGER

Schwarzenegger was the perfect physical specimen to play the musclebound Conan—and when the $100 million success of *Conan the Barbarian* led to a sequel, he was clearly in danger of becoming permanently typecast.

FROM BARBARIAN TO TERMINATOR

The intention was obviously to lighten the mood of the piece, keeping it more in line with what the studio perceived as a comic-book picture, something that obviously satisfied Arnold. "Even in the Conan days I wanted to do something funny." *Variety* thought he was already there— "As Conan, Arnold Schwarzenegger seems more animated and much funnier under Fleischer's direction then he did under John Milius in the original—he even has an amusing drunk scene."

While not all the reviews were as favourable as this one, *Conan the Destroyer* opened in July 1984, touted as a big summer blockbuster, and once again proved a significant hit with the public, eventually equalling

> **"Even in the Conan days I wanted to do something funny."**
> **Arnold Schwarzenegger**

Arnold looks forward to the day when he can leave his loincloth behind.

The Terminator (1984) was the first movie to feature Schwarzenegger prominently as a brand name.

"*The Terminator* automatically doubled my price."
Arnold Schwarzenegger

the original film's worldwide gross of over $100 million (£67 million).

Terminal bad guy
Although hard to imagine now, taking the title role in *The Terminator* was something of a risk for Arnold at the time. While conscious of building his heroic image with the public, he had to play an extremely violent, heartless killing machine. But it was to prove the defining move of his film career, and turned him into a megastar. "*The Terminator* automatically doubled my price," he later said.

Filming in March 1984, four months before the release of *Conan the Destroyer*, it was clear from the start that this was going to be something special. Co-written by the husband-and-wife team of James Cameron and Gale Anne Hurd, whose company was responsible for such films as *The Abyss*, this unique science-fiction thriller was to be fully realized by the emerging genius of director Cameron.

FROM BARBARIAN TO TERMINATOR

Seen by many as a religious parable—Michael Biehn as Kyle Reese returns from the devastation of Los Angeles in 2028 to the twentieth century to protect the mother of an unborn child who is destined to be the saviour of mankind—*The Terminator* was a genre classic that pleased the science-fiction purists and crossed over to a populist audience. In its breathtaking imagination and nightmarish vision, it stands alongside Ridley Scott's *Blade Runner* as one of the best science-fiction movies of the Eighties.

The Terminator: ruthless and unstoppable.

Arnold the unstoppable
Cameron called the nightclub in his movie "TechNoir", but he might just as easily have been describing his distinctive visual aesthetic. His film is hardware heavy, seriously dark in tone, frenetic,

> "I'll be back."
> Arnold Schwarzenegger as the Terminator

stylish and steeped in violence and horror, and it uses the sheer physical prowess of Schwarzenegger as the object of fear. Here was Arnold the perfect body turned indestructible killing machine: cold, unreasonable, unstoppable. Cameron played with our deepest fears about the bodybuilding giant: what if all that power and strength was directed

ARNOLD SCHWARZENEGGER

James Cameron's tech-noir thriller turned Arnold into a world superstar.

against us, how could we stop it? One critic described it as "the greatest horror performance since Boris Karloff".

Strangely enough, the inhuman nature of the beast gave Arnold what was not only his most appropriate but also his most rounded role to date.

FROM BARBARIAN TO TERMINATOR

The Terminator gave him a chance to forsake his loincloth and look cool and menacing in leather and shades, and he developed his first humorous catchphrase: the monotonic "I'll be back" became the most popular and frequently quoted line from any of his movies, and was knowingly used as the only line of dialogue years later for the advance trailers for *Terminator 2: Judgment Day*.

You look familiar...

Arnie the brand name
The Terminator also saw Arnold's surname being prominently used for the first time in the movie's advertising. "It was like letting the industry know we don't have to sell muscles—now we can just sell Arnold." It was an approach that worked. The single surname "Schwarzenegger" has featured prominently on the posters and advertising for all his subsequent movies, like a brand name, a sign of quality and reassurance for the audience. Never mind what it's about—it's a "Schwarzenegger" movie.

The Terminator was released in the autumn of 1984 to universal acclaim. "*The Terminator* is a blazing, cinematic comic book, full of virtuoso movie-making, terrific momentum, solid performances and a compelling story," wrote

> **"It was like letting the industry know we don't have to sell muscles—now we can just sell Arnold."**
> **Arnold Schwarzenegger**

ARNOLD SCHWARZENEGGER

On the set of Red Sonja (1985) Arnold fulfils his contractual obligations with Brigitte Nielsen, the future Mrs Sylvester Stallone.

Opposite page and overleaf: If all else fails, just use a bigger gun—Commando (1985).

one critic, going on to say, "The shotgun-wielding Schwarzenegger is perfectly cast in a machine-like portrayal that requires only a few lines of dialogue."

Time magazine placed the film on its prestigious list of the top ten films of the year, while the Avoriaz Film Festival in France presented it with its Grand Prix award. This critical acclaim was more than matched by box-office receipts. Grossing in excess of $65 million (£43.3 million) in the US alone, it quickly surpassed the success of *Conan the Destroyer*, released a few months before, as audiences responded eagerly to Schwarzenegger's brutal anti-hero. Even sales of the brand of sunglasses he sports for the majority of the movie boomed on the back of the film's success. The popularity of both this and the *Conan* sequel led the National Association of Theatre Owners to name Arnold the International Star of 1984 at their ShoWest convention in Las Vegas that year.

Seeing red
Though eager to capitalize on his most successful year to date in movies, Arnold was temporarily prevented from following up *Terminator*. A contractual obligation to Dino De Laurentiis saw him back on location in Italy filming *Red Sonja*.

FROM BARBARIAN TO TERMINATOR

Red Sonja was De Laurentiis's way of trying to build on the *Conan* success, this time with a female character. For the title role he had discovered and cast former model Brigitte Nielsen, a tall Amazonian blonde, who would later marry and very publicly divorce Arnold's screen rival Sylvester Stallone. Based once again on a character created by Robert E. Howard, and with Richard Fleischer returning to the director's chair, *Red Sonja* was a brief but not damaging aberration in Arnold's career.

Commanding attention
Early 1985 saw Arnold back in Hollywood and starring in a striking action movie, *Commando*, which was designed to capitalize on his recent success. Rae Dawn Chong was the wisecracking sidekick, and producer Joel Silver was hoping to re-create the balance of humour and action of his blockbuster *48 Hours*.

For Arnold, *Commando* offered the perfect opportunity to display more than the icy cold inhumanity

ARNOLD SCHWARZENEGGER

FROM BARBARIAN TO TERMINATOR

of *The Terminator*. "In the beginning of this film I play a loving, gentle and understanding father to my daughter Jenny. I educate her and protect her. Then she's kidnapped and I immediately have to snap back into the personality many associate with *The Terminator* and *Conan* films. I become a fighting machine that will not stop until my objective is completed. But between the loving father and the machine, I have to deal with this character, Cindy (Rae Dawn Chong), who is always giving me a dirty look or a funny line in response to whatever I say. The relationship with Cindy works as comic relief, and it adds another dimension to the character."

The humorous side of Arnold's character was something he would continue to develop on screen, and which helped to separate him from the other action stars of the day. It had been part of his image as early as *Pumping Iron*, and director Mark Lester was quick to exploit it. "It's easy to fall into a trap about Arnold's abilities when you consider his previous films and his physique. But he has this incredible sense of humour and it goes all day. So we brought that element, Arnold's natural humour, into the film."

Shooting on location around LA, Arnold opted to do most of his stunts himself, and

ARNOLD SCHWARZENEGGER

> "It's easy to fall into a trap about Arnold's abilities when you consider his previous films and his physique. But he has this incredible sense of humour and it goes all day."
>
> **Mark Lester**

incurred a dislocated shoulder and stitches in his hand and elbow from jumping through windows and hanging on to the landing gear of a plane among other recreational activities. His director was quick to praise him. "There's nobody else but Arnold who could have done what he did. I've made 15 pictures, and he's the only actor who has ever done the kind of action that we've done."

Pressing engagement

Shooting on *Commando* concluded on July 3. Just over a month later, Arnold announced his engagement to Maria Shriver. Since they had first met in 1977, Arnold and Maria had been constant

FROM BARBARIAN TO TERMINATOR

companions. Despite the political differences of the liberal Kennedys and the staunch Republican Schwarzenegger, his friendship with her family, in particular with her mother Eunice Shriver, had led to Arnold's further involvement with numerous charitable organizations, most notably Eunice's pet project, the Special Olympics, a sporting event for the physically and mentally handicapped. Arnold had become National Weight Training Coach for the event.

Partly spurred on by Arnold's intense drive, Maria was finding success in her

Arnold and Maria announced their engagement in August 1985.

> "There's nobody else but Arnold who could have done what he did. I've made 15 pictures, and he's the only actor who has ever done the kind of action that we've done."
> **Mark Lester**

ARNOLD SCHWARZENEGGER

own career as a TV news presenter, realizing her ambition of becoming an anchor person before the age of 30, on *CBS Morning News*. Long the perfect media couple—the brawny movie star, the cerebral news woman; the self-made American icon, the child born to America's first family—Arnold and Maria made their engagement official on August 10. Although he was based on the west coast, and her TV career kept her in New York most of the time, shortly after the engagement Arnold nevertheless bought a mansion in Pacific Palisades, in preparation for marriage and family life.

A certain light touch

Commando opened in October, providing Arnold with another hit, proving once again that his instincts for his career—the underscoring of his action persona with comedy—was what both the audience and the critics wanted to see. "In *Commando*, the fetching surprise is the glancing humour between the quixotic and larky Rae Dawn Chong and the straight-faced killing machine of Arnold Schwarzenegger," opined *Variety*. "Chong lights up the

FROM BARBARIAN TO TERMINATOR

film like a firefly, Schwarzenegger delivers a certain light touch of his own, the result is palatable action comics."

Commando was one of the top-grossing films of the year, and this time earned Arnold the ShoWest's Career Achievement Award.

Raw Deal

Never one to rest on his laurels, and mindful of the need to steer his career to an even higher peak—Stallone, courtesy of *Rambo: First Blood II*, was still commanding a bigger paycheck than him and remained a Reagan-era icon—Schwarzenegger was back before the cameras within the month, filming *Raw Deal*.

Arnold chose *Raw Deal* in part, again, to develop his career and screen image; the role of a former FBI man reinstated to infiltrate Chicago's biggest mob family offered Arnold the opportunity to concentrate more on his acting ability than on his physical assets. Arnold was still keen to move beyond anything that could limit him in his quest for movie megastardom. He was sensitive to what he had led his fans to expect—"I would never alienate people by denying them the things they have come to see me for in the past. I got my breaks in the business because of my physical attributes. What I have done in this film [*Raw Deal*], and will continue to do, is to add on new facets to the characters that I play, exposing new sides of myself." However, he did hope that: "Eventually down the

Jean Claude Van Damme, a pretender to Arnold's action-hero throne.

ARNOLD SCHWARZENEGGER

line, I'll play a role where the physical and athletic skills aren't necessary."

In the mouth of such great pretenders as Jean Claude Van Damme or Chuck Norris, these words would have appeared little more than wishful thinking and publicity hyperbole. But coming from Arnold, it was clear that he meant it. He viewed the movies as a competitive sport, and he would not rest until he was the biggest star in the world. With *Raw Deal* finished and his wedding to Maria set for the following April, Arnold used the intervening time to travel to Puerto Vallarta to film the science-fiction action movie *Predator*.

Predator

One element that constantly distinguishes Schwarzenegger's screen career is his ability to associate himself with emergent talent. On *The Terminator* he formed an alliance with James Cameron, whose subsequent work on *Aliens* and *The Abyss* would make him one of Hollywood's most unique, ambitious and sought-after directors. On *Commando*, Arnold teamed with producer Joel Silver, already successful on the strength of *48 Hours*, but who over the next few years would become a modern

It may just be a rescue mission, but this soldier is taking no chances: *Predator* (1987).

FROM BARBARIAN TO TERMINATOR

Hollywood legend, the ultimate action producer, busting budgets and box-office records with the *Die Hard* movies, *Last Boy Scout*, the *Lethal Weapon* series and others.

Predator was a breakthrough film for director John McTiernan, an exciting, visceral action talent, who would soon rise to compete with James Cameron as Hollywood's leading hardware director, redefining the action genre with *Die Hard* and *The Hunt for Red October*.

Predator combined the elements of Arnold's most successful movies to date: the militarily spiced action of *Commando* with the science-fiction background of *Terminator*. Head of an élite covert operations team sent on a rescue mission, Arnold (nicknamed "Dutch", probably to explain the accent) is trapped in a hostile jungle as his men are hunted and picked off one by one by a chameleon-like and mostly invisible alien being.

The Austrian Oak faces an invisible enemy alien in *Predator* (1987).

ARNOLD SCHWARZENEGGER

Commando Arnold ponders: a bullet or a one-liner?

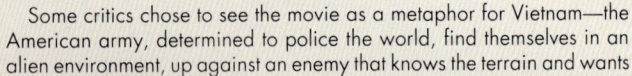

Some critics chose to see the movie as a metaphor for Vietnam—the American army, determined to police the world, find themselves in an alien environment, up against an enemy that knows the terrain and wants them out. But *Predator* chiefly showcased two things: the action skills of producer Silver and director McTiernan, and the screen heroism of its star, Arnold Schwarzenegger.

Director McTiernan was impressed with Arnold's acting skills, telling one newspaper reporter: "The range of things he can do is expanding daily...The guy could be another John Wayne."

A line in wit

As well as confirming Arnold's status as top action hero, the film reinforced what was to become one of his trademarks: a blackly comic quip after each act of violence ("Stick around" he says to the guy he's just nailed to the wall, for example). This was not an original trait for an action hero—the comparatively tame James Bond had been doing it for years—but it was an important one for Arnold, as it

> **"The range of things he can do is expanding daily...The guy could be another John Wayne."**
> **John McTiernan**

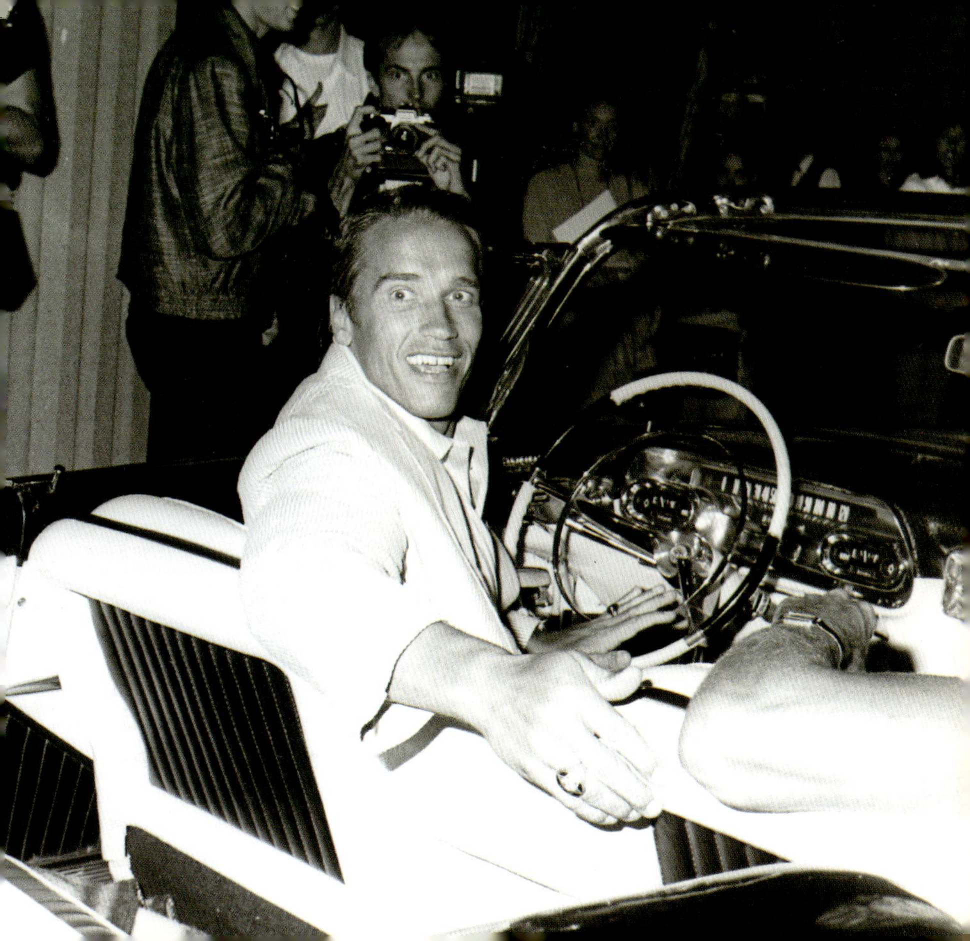

ARNOLD SCHWARZENEGGER

Gearing up for the celebrity wedding of the decade.

Previous page: At the première of James Cameron's Aliens (1986).

reminded the audience that he was a comic-book hero and not a violent thug, and that his exploits were performed in the spirit of entertainment.

It was a trait that every screen action star of recent years has attempted to employ, though few have done it with more success or aplomb than Arnold. In 1988, critic David Denby offered his thoughts on the secret of this success, which he felt, in fact, had little to do with talent or intent: "Most of all he's a star because of his voice—the sound, the accent, the emphasis. It's what everyone remembers and imitates. To Americans a French or Italian accent may be charming or irritating, but a German accent is almost invariably funny."

Superstar wedding

On April 26, 1986, Arnold returned from filming *Predator* to marry Maria Shriver, which many saw as the ultimate sign of his Americanization—acceptance into the closest thing America has to a Royal Family, the Kennedys. Long-time friend and fellow bodybuilder Franco Columbu was best man. The wedding was held at the Church of St Francis Xavier, near the Kennedy estate in Hyannis Port. The reception that followed was marred only by the presence of a gift from Austrian president Kurt Waldheim, for whom Arnold had previously pledged support, but who had subsequently been linked to wartime Nazi activities.

The couple honeymooned in Antigua.

> **"Stick around."**
> **Arnold Schwarzenegger**
> **in *Predator***

Divide and conquer

With two movies ready for release, and the perfect marriage made, the immigrant had found acceptance into the heart of America. But for the ever-competitive Arnold it was not enough. His career and his highly public life were like a muscle, constantly needing to be pumped and developed. With his asking price for a movie now at $10 million (£6.7 million), it seemed things could hardly improve. But Arnold knew that in the affluent Eighties, his movies could get bigger, his salaries could get bigger, and his audience could get bigger. He had proved that he had a loyal audience, and his all-action movies were hits. So now Arnold wanted to make movies that appealed to everyone—the wider the appeal, the larger the audience, and the greater the success. As he had demonstrated in his business dealings, diversification was the key.

CHAPTER 4

Total Stardom

"It's hard to do heroic films and bring out vulnerability," Arnold said, as the rest of 1986 saw a slow but distinct move away from the ultimately limited area of the action genre.

Raw Deal opened in June 1986, to the now predictable results of a strong box office and a lacklustre critical reception. Arnold knew that to progress, he had to cross over, find a way of moving from the male-dominated action-genre audience to the general mass market and attract new fans—especially the young adult female market—while not alienating the old.

Arnold and co-star Yaphet Kotto in the costumes that mark them out as human targets in *The Running Man* (1987).

TOTAL STARDOM

The Running Man (1987) was based on a book by Stephen King, writing under his pseudonym Richard Bachman.

His most recent movies had been calculated, though not always successful, attempts to do that. *Raw Deal* allowed his character to work within a family situation while still delivering the goods on the action side. The upcoming *Predator* reunited him with the science-fiction audience of

ARNOLD SCHWARZENEGGER

The Terminator and also kept the action quota high. For his next movie he would attempt to combine all these elements.

The Running Man
The Running Man, which had the distinct commercial advantage of being adapted from a book by Richard Bachman (Stephen King's recently revealed pseudonym), was a science-fiction action movie that relied heavily on humour and satire. As a career move, it seemed a step back for Arnold. Having aligned himself with the new generation of Hollywood talent, Arnold now donned a tacky leotard and left himself in the workmanlike hands of director Paul Michael Glaser, best known for his starring role in the popular Seventies TV show *Starsky and Hutch*.

With a budget of $27 million (£18 million), filming began on this futuristic tale of TV's most popular and lethal game show in September 1986. Wrongly imprisoned, Arnold's Ben Richards is picked to be a contestant on *The Running Man*, and is hunted through the post-nuclear ruins of a once-great city by a group of varied assailants known as Stalkers, in what is basically a cross between *Rollerball* and *American Gladiators*.

There was a lot to enjoy in *The Running Man*, from the casting of Richard Dawson, host of the popular US TV show *Family Feud*, as *The Running Man*'s callous host, to the variety of background TV satire. But while it allowed Arnold the opportunity for more black humour—including "I'll be back" in knowing reference to himself—*The Running Man*, though popular at the box office, was not really the quality of picture that Arnold wanted to pursue. Notably he did the least amount of publicity for it of any of his recent movies.

Walking star
1987 saw Arnold's star ascending—in June he was awarded his own star on the Hollywood Boulevard Walk of Fame. Both he and Maria

attended the ceremony of this, the 1,847th star awarded.

A few days later, *Predator* opened to some of the best returns of Arnold's career, proving a major summer hit and becoming one of the top-grossing films of the year. *The Running Man* rode in on that success in November, providing another sizeable box-office hit. The two movies combined prompted the National Association of Theatre Owners to give Schwarzenegger its Star of the Year Award.

Russian buddy

Arnold's next movie was to prove his most overt move yet towards the longed-for crossover. Although *Red Heat* became his least commercially successful film since *Red Sonja*, it found him back working with an established director, Walter Hill (*48 Hours*, *The Warriors*, *Southern Comfort*), and working in the newly successful genre of the "buddy picture". Since teaming Eddie Murphy with Nick Nolte had led to the enormous success of *48 Hours*, and Mel Gibson and Danny Glover had developed a licence to print money with *Lethal Weapon*, the concept of the star double-act, a crowd-pleasing blend of comedy and action, was the latest Hollywood vogue.

Arnold receives the 1,847th star on the Hollywood Boulevard Walk of Fame.

ARNOLD SCHWARZENEGGER

"There were two reasons why we were approved to film in Moscow. First, the changing political climate—*glasnost*—and second, Arnold Schwarzenegger—the fact that he plays a Russian hero."

Walter Hill

Schwarzenegger seemed a natural for this, and was teamed with James Belushi, for the first time in his career sharing equal billing on the poster and advertising—although Belushi was paid considerably less than Arnold's current fee of $10 million (£6.7 million).

Deadpan Danko

With his *Red Heat* role as Russian police Captain Ivan Danko, Schwarzenegger found both a perfect vehicle for his heavily accented voice and a part that allowed him to play on the deadpan side of his humour. It was also an example of his ability to tap into the current *Zeitgeist*—in the era of developing *glasnost* and the end of the Cold War, Arnold's character showed the audience the human side beneath the grim exterior of the Russian people.

"Ivan Danko is a very intelligent guy. But when he gets sent to Chicago to extradite a Russian drug-dealer against whom he has a personal vendetta, it's like he's wearing blinders. Little by little though, mainly through the American policeman assigned to him, he learns things about the American way that he takes home with him."

ARNOLD SCHWARZENEGGER

Never one to miss a photo opportunity, Arnold sends along a waxwork double to please the press.

Previous pages: Arnold as Ivan Danko in Red Heat (1988).

Red Heat became the first American movie to shoot in Red Square in Moscow. "There were two reasons why we were approved to film in Moscow," explained director Walter Hill. "First, the changing political climate—*glasnost*—and second, Arnold Schwarzenegger—the fact that he plays a Russian hero."

Hill was extremely keen to work with the Austrian superstar. "We'd known each other socially, and I'd always been impressed by Arnold as a screen presence. He's a larger-than-life hero in the classic tradition, capable of incredible feats of courage and daring. And personally Arnold's a self-made man, a quality that appeals to Americans. He's a self-made man in a more literal sense than anyone you'll ever know, because he literally made his own body as well as his career."

Arnold attacked his role with his customary appetite, studying Russian for three months prior to filming, and losing 10lbs (4.5kg) for the role, which, along with the 15lbs (7 kg) he had lost for *The Running Man*, had reduced him to slightly more human proportions. Along with its Moscow and Chicago locations, *Red Heat* filmed partly in Budapest—doubling for Russia—where Arnold shot the semi-naked snowbound fight that opens the movie. "He has a real sense of humour about himself," added Hill. "He would go out there and fight in the snow with no clothes on and never complain."

The production was marred, however, by one tragic event, when on February 6 Arnold's 54-year-old stuntman, Benny Dobbins, died abruptly of a heart attack.

TOTAL STARDOM

Red Heat stone cold

When the film opened the following summer, it proved to be only a moderate hit at the box office, but for Arnold it was a huge personal success. While Belushi's was ostensibly the comic role in the movie, Arnold played against him perfectly, upstaging him by using his supposed lack of humour as the focus of his comedy. As *Variety* noted, "Schwarzenegger, who, when he dons a green suit, is dubbed 'Gumby' by Belushi, is right on target with his characterization of the iron-willed soldier."

Red Heat may have lost its way at the summer box office, but Arnold was clearly finding his way. Blending his action-heavy persona into comedy was working, as he enthused at the time: "Comedy comes naturally to me. Even competing in sports, where everyone would get very intense, I could always joke about it. And I look forward, down the line, to doing straight comedy.".

Arnold may have been talking publicly of some time "down the line", but privately he knew the time was right. He had proved himself to be one of the leading action stars in the world, an effective part of a double act, and a screen hero with the ability to laugh at himself for the benefit of the audience. The

> "He has a real sense of humour about himself. He would go out there and fight in the snow with no clothes on and never complain."
> **Walter Hill**

The future chairman of the President's Council on Physical Fitness and Sports gets in shape.

groundwork had been laid over his last few movies; now was the time to make the move. That move arrived in the form of *Twins*.

Brotherly love
For his most important movie since finding barbarian-inspired success back in 1982, Arnold was taking no chances, and he carefully selected the best people for the job: in this case, director Ivan Reitman, whose previous successes included the phenomenal *Ghostbusters*.

It was Reitman, upon meeting his old friend Danny DeVito and Arnold in the same week, who hatched the idea of a comedy starring the two of them. Reitman told two British writers that he had met, William Osborne and William Davies, that he was looking for a vehicle for the two stars. The writers said they had a suitable outline back at their hotel and went off to get it. In fact, they went to the beach and came up with the inspired idea of making Arnold and Danny long-lost twins.

Twins worked perfectly as a concept. As Ivan Reitman once remarked, all you needed to see were the names "Schwarzenegger" and "DeVito" side by side with the title *Twins* and it said everything about the movie you ever needed to know. The plot—concerning genetic experiments and perfect Julius (Schwarzenegger) coming to America to find his long-lost and genetically impure brother

"Only their mother can tell them apart."—*Twins* (1988)

TOTAL STARDOM

Vincent (DeVito)—was extraneous. At a time when cinema was dominated by such "high concepts", *Twins* was about as high as you could get without a pilot's licence.

"In my last five or six films", said Arnold, "my love relationship was basically with guns, explosives, grenades and missiles. This was for me a learning experience all the way through, especially when it comes to comedy, timing and all those things."

Filming took place in the spring of 1988, immediately following *Red Heat*, and offered Arnold his first on-screen love scene, with co-star Kelly Preston. At the time he joked about the situation: "When you're my age, and when you're married, that's the only way you can get close to a girl, when you have a scene like that." Director Reitman, however, though he was impressed with Arnold's acting ability and his obvious range, nevertheless had some

The unlikely pairing of Arnold and Danny was a box-office smash hit.

> **"Comedy comes naturally to me. Even competing in sports, where everyone would get very intense, I could always joke about it."**
> **Arnold Schwarzenegger**

ARNOLD SCHWARZENEGGER

Danny DeVito shapes up alongside Arnold and heavyweight champ Mike Tyson.

problems in directing him, achieving his post-coital expression in the love scene by literally directing his facial reaction muscle by muscle. "He has extraordinary physical control," said Reitman. "And it extends to his face."

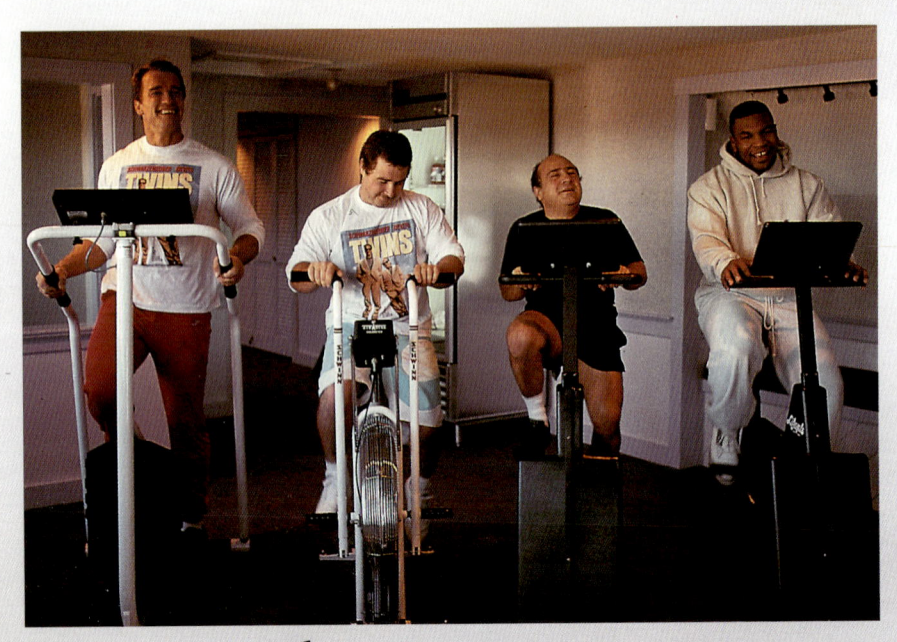

Arnold gets ready for his first on-screen love scene with *Twins* co-star Kelly Preston.

Crossing over

The obvious fear for both Arnold and the studio backing him in this move away from his traditional cinematic fare was that while he might well attract a new audience, his old one might feel betrayed and leave him behind. This was not to be the case with *Twins*, which proved to be the crossover vehicle its star always knew it would be. "They made a test of the movie and the real hard-core Arnold audience felt that this was the best movie I've ever done," he said. "It shows frustrations. It shows ups and downs. A lot of love and caring."

Twins opened on December 5, 1988 to universal acclaim. One critic enthused: "Schwarzenegger is a delightful surprise in this perfect transitional role to comedy. So strongly does he project the tenderness, nobility and puppy-dog devotion that make Julius tick that one is nearly

ARNOLD SCHWARZENEGGER

Arnold and *Twins* co-star Danny DeVito celebrate Arnold's first on-screen love scene.

> "The force of a family is the strongest force there is, the greatest support you can have, the greatest love that can be given."
> **Arnold Schwarzenegger**

hypnotized into suspending disbelief." *Twins* became the hit of the Christmas season, eventually grossing over $111 million (£74 million) in the States alone. President-elect George Bush, for whom Arnold had campaigned in the recent election, attended the celebrity première.

A good deal of the success of *Twins* obviously lies in the chemistry of Schwarzenegger and DeVito, and the loyalty of Arnold's fans, but a good deal must also be attributed to Arnold's ability to gauge the desires of the American people. With Reagan, the most popular President in recent history, only recently de-throned, the country was still steeped in Reagan's vision of an apple-pie country, a place where emphasis on such values as family and loyalty were dominant. Arnold knew how, and more importantly when, to tap into this. "The force of a family is the strongest force there is, the greatest support you can have, the greatest love that can be given. Julius and Vincent can give that to one another."

TOTAL STARDOM

With its two major stars and big-name director Reitman involved, *Twins* had always been seen as a huge investment on the part of a studio. In order to keep costs relatively low in an era of spiralling budgets and salaries—spurred on, of course, by Arnold and his $10 million (£6.7 million) basic take-home pay—all three participants had agreed to defer their payments in favour of a percentage of the box office take, with Arnold in line for 17.5% of the overall gross—not bad for a movie that saw him emerge as Hollywood's hottest property.

The money made from *Twins* helped make Arnold the sixth highest-earning entertainer of the year according to *Forbes* magazine: he earned $35 million (£23.3 million)—compared to a mere $29 million (£19.3 million) the previous year—which placed him one position behind his old rival Sylvester Stallone.

Arnold had once again set himself a goal and surpassed it. His only choice now was to go further. His fee for his next film, *Total Recall,* was both the standard $10 million (£6.7 million) *and* a percentage of the profits.

Courtside with Maria and talk-show host Arsenio Hall.

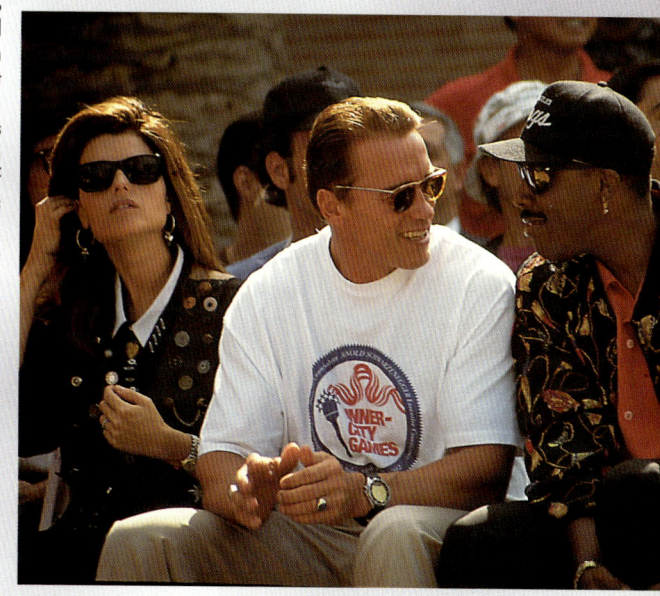

ARNOLD SCHWARZENEGGER

Arnold and Danny opted for a percentage of the profits from *Twins* rather than a fee. The film went on to gross close to $200 million (£133 million).

Opposite page: **The futuristic *Total Recall* began as a short story by *Blade Runner* author Philip K. Dick.**

Total Recall
Based on a short story, "We Can Remember It For You Wholesale", by science-fiction author Philip K. Dick (another of his short stories had served as the inspiration for *Blade Runner*), the screenplay for *Total Recall*, by *Alien* writers Dan O'Bannon and Ronald Shusett, had knocked around Hollywood for the best part of a decade, at various points set to be made by David Cronenberg with Richard Dreyfuss in the lead, and later with Bruce Beresford helming and Patrick Swayze starring.

Arnold could see in the script an opportunity for a first-class action adventure movie: "The reason I was interested in *Total Recall* for so many years is that it had twists in the story that action movies don't usually have. With this story I had to read through to the last page to know the whole thing."

Having assaulted the box office with his crowd-pleasing *Robocop*, which combined graphic violence in a futuristic world with a man-is-better-than-machine storyline and a few moments of grim humour, Dutch director Paul Verhoeven was a natural choice for the next Schwarzenegger movie. Arnold compared him to the other great action directors he had worked with. "Jim Cameron, John McTiernan and Paul Verhoeven. These three guys are very much alike. They want to be part of the action rather than sitting in a chair and directing."

TOTAL STARDOM

87

ARNOLD SCHWARZENEGGER

Sharon Stone became the first woman to kick Arnie's butt on-screen in *Total Recall* (1990).

Verhoeven may have been in (or out of) the director's chair, but *Total Recall* was Arnold's project right from the start. *Premiere* magazine termed it "a $50 million [£33.3 million] manifestation of Hollywood star power—power he has taken to the bank". As well as choosing his director, Arnold was involved in all aspects of casting, marketing and pre-sales, and had persuaded Carolco pictures to buy the script in the first place. Arnold's dedication to the film was total: "You can scream at me, call me for a shot at midnight, keep me waiting for hours," he said. "As

TOTAL STARDOM

long as what ends up on the screen is perfect." Shooting began on March 20, 1989, at the Churubusco Studios in Mexico City, where sets were created to represent Earth in the year 2084 and the now colonized Mars, where Doug Quaid (Schwarzenegger) travels to learn his real identity. Arnold explained the premise of the film.

"Doug Quaid is a very normal kind of guy who works in construction but actually has another life that was deprogrammed from his mind. When he's confronted with this information, he doesn't know what his reality is and what is nothing more than a programmed dream. The audience will not know either, and that's what makes this movie so very interesting."

Just an ordinary working guy—or is he? Arnold in *Total Recall* (1990).

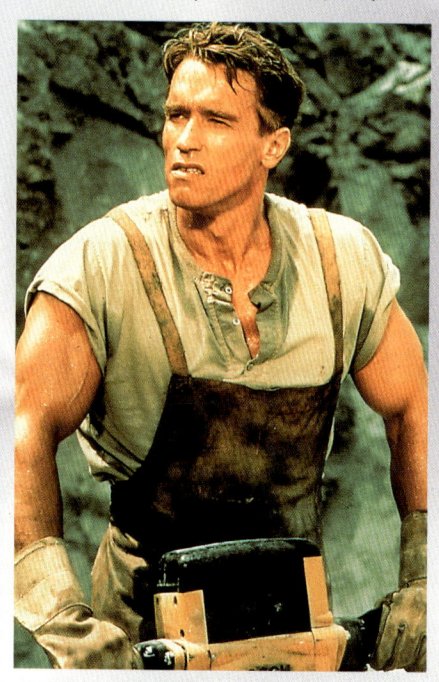

Mex-up

Filming in Mexico City was hazardous to most of the cast and crew's health, and various bouts of food poisoning did not help the atmosphere on

> **"You can scream at me, call me for a shot at midnight, keep me waiting for hours. As long as what ends up on the screen is perfect."**
> **Arnold Schwarzenegger**

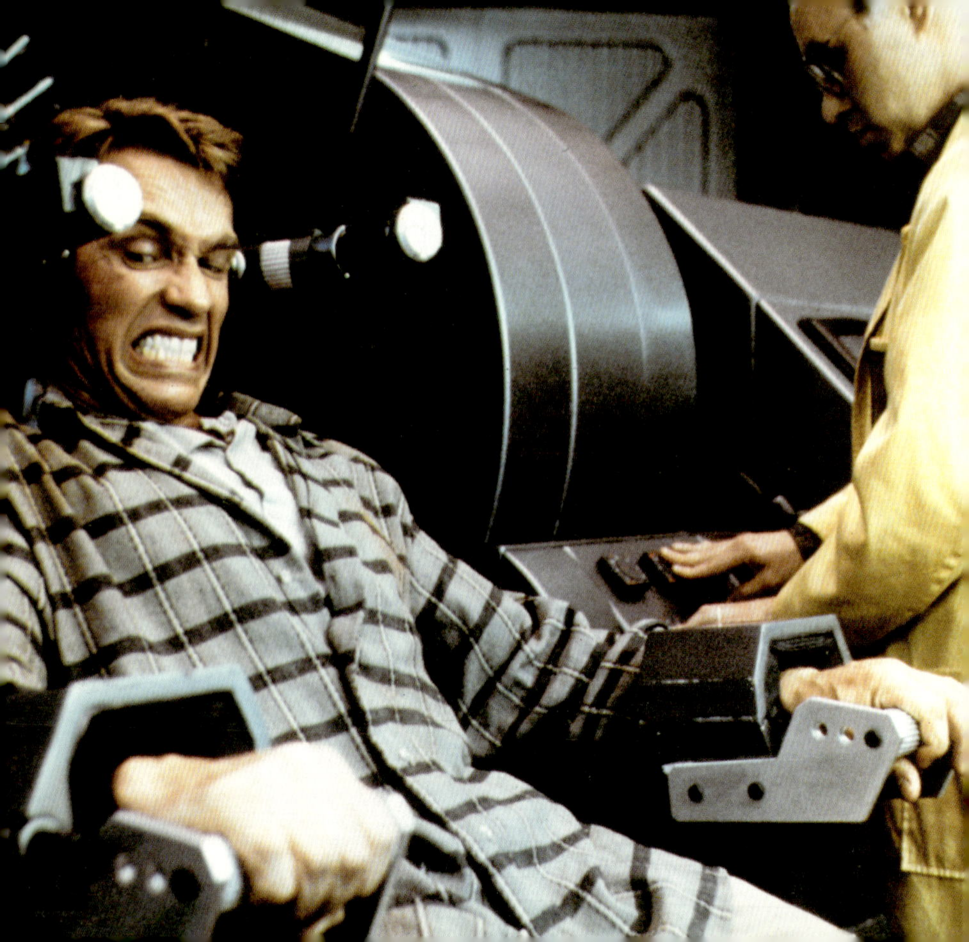

TOTAL STARDOM

the lengthy five-month shoot. Arnold escaped illness, reportedly because he had his personal assistant scrub all fruits and vegetables before his food was cooked.

Reports of Verhoeven's outbursts on the set became rife during production, and Arnold took on the role of peacemaker: "I'm always there to pull things together, pour a thimbleful of schnapps, put on the Austrian music, cheer things up and keep everyone on track." Even though it was feared that the level of violence in the movie would earn it an unmarketable X rating in the US, Arnold flexed a little executive muscle to ensure the director was allowed to work: "I'm a strong believer in the director being the most important thing of the movie."

Paul Verhoeven himself said at the time: "Without Arnold, this movie would have been a real hell to go through. If he likes the director and he thinks he's doing a good job, then he supports

> "I'm a strong believer in the director being the most important thing of the movie."
> **Arnold Schwarzenegger**

ARNOLD SCHWARZENEGGER

As chairman of President Bush's Council for Physical Fitness and Sports, Arnold toured the country to promote physical fitness among the young.

him as I have never seen an actor do. Because Arnold is more than an actor, he's a very socially gifted guy." Even so, Arnold encouraged Verhoeven to film softer footage in some of the more explicit scenes.

Arnold the fat lady

Arnold claimed that this would be the first movie where "you see me travelling to Mars as a 300-pound fat lady". For this element alone, it deserved nothing but the best in marketing. Around $70 million (£46.6 million) was invested in its production, and anything up to an additional $30 million (£20 million) was set aside to promote the movie, with Arnold involved in every stage. "I'm a marketing freak," he said, well aware of the need to prepare everything meticulously ahead of time. "It's important to get everyone psyched up a year in advance."

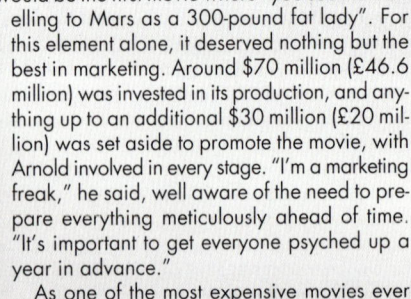

As one of the most expensive movies ever made by that time, *Total Recall* was an extreme act of faith in its star on behalf of the studios involved. The critical response seemed to be more than favourable, with *Empire* magazine calling it "the first great science-fiction movie of the Nineties".

Total Recall was released in the summer of 1990 and earned $25 million (£16.6 million) in its first weekend. It was one of the major hits of the year, and proved to be Arnold's biggest film to date, establishing him once and for all as the biggest action star in the world.

TOTAL STARDOM

Media darling

As successful as Arnold's film career now was, he still took time to work on his other role, that of media socialite. The birth to Arnold and Maria of their first child, Katherine Eunice, on December 13, 1989 ensured numerous television chat-show appearances for Arnold, extolling the wonders of fatherhood.

In March of the same year Arnold established the Arnold Schwarzenegger Classic, a bodybuilding contest offering the lure of big prize money, something that had not been available when Arnold had begun his own career years before.

And then, of course, there was the President. A long-time supporter of Ronald Reagan, Conan the Republican was now also a good friend of President George Bush, having campaigned for him in the 1988 election, as he would again in his 1992 defeat to Bill Clinton. Arnold's loyalty was rewarded in 1990, when President Bush appointed him chairman of the President's Council on Physical Fitness and Sports, which saw Arnold touring the country, publicly promoting physical fitness among the young, in what many saw once again as a precursor to his future political career. He jokingly sent up this role in a cameo appearance in Ivan Reitman's 1993 hit *Dave*.

The business side of Arnold's life was equally busy. With long-time rival Sylvester Stallone's star now on the wane, after he had tried to follow Arnold's example and move into comedy with

Arnold and Maria with their daughter Katherine Eunice.

ARNOLD SCHWARZENEGGER

Conan the Republican gets George Bush jogging for the Great American Workout, May 1991.

such vehicles as *Oscar* and *Stop! Or My Mom Will Shoot*, Arnold could now relinquish the battle and go into business with Sly. Having seen the worldwide success of the Hard Rock Café chain, Arnold joined forces with Stallone and *Die Hard* star Bruce Willis to open a series of restaurants called Planet Hollywood, themed around the movies. The three action stars co-own the Planet Hollywood chain, but despite the

TOTAL STARDOM

inclusion of such personal items on the menu as Arnold's mother's strudel, they are largely seen as figureheads, lending their public profile and panache to a highly profitable business enterprise.

Kindergarten Cop

Having blasted everyone to gory pieces over the summer, Arnold now decided that Christmas was the time for comedy and kids. Hence he re-teamed with *Twins* director Ivan Reitman for *Kindergarten Cop*.

As with his previous comedy outing, the idea was simple—take Arnie's big-screen strongman character and stick him in a roomful of adorable pre-school kids. "The character I play goes through a complete transformation," Arnold said during production. "At first he's a cop who knows

Arnold, Sylvester Stallone and Bruce Willis celebrate the opening of another branch of their upmarket burger joint, Planet Hollywood.

only one thing—his job...And then all of a sudden he goes undercover and has the painful experience of facing 30 children in the classroom with absolutely no idea how to communicate with them. It changes him completely."

Kindergarten Cop was released at Christmas 1990 to mixed reviews—"It's supposed to be funny to have this grim, musclebound control freak confronted with five-year olds he can't intimidate, but it isn't"—and something of a disappointing box office—$54 million (£36 million) in the States. The film was generally criticized for bringing too much realistic violence to what was essentially a family movie. *Home Alone*, which opened at the same time, relied heavily on violence of a cartoon nature, and although that was not without its critics, it seemed more acceptable to parents and more appealing to children, and the film went on to gross in excess of $220 million (£140 million) that Christmas.

Despite the mediocre success of *Kindergarten Cop*, Arnold did his usual amount of publicity in selling the film. In one major interview, with *Empire* magazine, he discussed his overview of his career and ambitions to date.

TOTAL STARDOM

> "I had to be realistic. Here I was, this bodybuilding champion. What could I do? Well, I could use my assets. I had a personality and a great body... I sold many tickets that way. Then I began to put more and more comic relief into my movies. I had to bring the people slowly with me."
>
> **Arnold Schwarzenegger**

Arnold goes undercover and back to school—*Kindergarten Cop* (1990).

ARNOLD SCHWARZENEGGER

Arnold reveals his softer side in *Kindergarten Cop*.

"If I had my choice I would've made a *Kindergarten Cop* from day one, but I had to be realistic. Here I was, this bodybuilding champion. What could I do? Well, I could use my assets. I had a personality and a great body...I sold many tickets that way. Then I began to put more and more comic relief into my movies. I had to bring the people slowly

TOTAL STARDOM

with me...But I had faith in myself. That is one thing I have. And when you have a very clear vision of something, you will reach your goals. I had a very clear vision when I was 15 that I would be the world champion in bodybuilding. And when I was in the film *Stay Hungry* years ago, I said to myself, 'There is Clint Eastwood up there and Charles Bronson and Warren Beatty, so why not me too? It seems pretty empty up there so why not me too? There is room for one more. I can squeeze in there.' It was totally up to me to sell the public on the fact that I was now an actor and not a bodybuilding champion."

Power is everything

When *Premiere* published its first industry power list of the 100 most important players in Hollywood in 1990, Arnold had ranked twentieth, the third highest actor placing behind Tom Cruise and Eddie Murphy. His listing noted that he would be "a savvy producer if he doesn't run for governor instead". Though *Kindergarten Cop* was perceived as a disappointment by some, it was not seen so by the industry, and Arnold's standing improved. *Premiere*'s 1991 "Power In Hollywood" list saw Arnold rise to thirteenth position, the highest-ranked performer, and it listed his strengths as "stardom, brains, versatility, ambition...great tireless self-promoter".

Arnold now found himself in a unique position, not only in Hollywood, but in Hollywood history, claiming to be in demand for sequels to any one of at least five of his previous movies—*The Terminator*, *Predator*, *Commando*, *Twins* and *Total Recall*. Some, like *Commando 2*, were already in development; others, like *Predator 2* and the proposed sequel to *Total Recall*, would be made without his involvement.

As early as 1989, Arnold had been trying to make a movie adaptation of the comic hero *Sgt. Rock*, at one point saying that it would star all three Planet Hollywood owners: Stallone, Willis, and Schwarzenegger.

Terminator 2: Judgment Day (1991) was the movie all Arnie fans had been waiting for. The Terminator turns good guy to protect the young John Connor (Edward Furlong).

But the script still eluded him. Another long-held pet project, *Duke and Fluffy*, in which Arnold would play a dog transformed into a human, also wasn't working out.

Instead, he turned to the movie everyone wanted. *The Terminator* was still regarded, by fans and critics alike, as Arnold's best movie. After all, he had said "I'll be back," and everyone was waiting. By 1991, the wait was finally over, as James Cameron's groundbreaking, visionary epic *Terminator 2: Judgment Day* became the most expensive film ever made and Arnold's biggest ever hit.

TOTAL STARDOM

He's back!

Arnold's meteoric career rise since the original *Terminator* in 1984 had proved to him one thing that led to a major change in this sequel—he was now too big a star to risk playing a bad guy. Consequently his killer cyborg was turned into the saviour of the movie, sent back to protect John Connor (Edward Furlong), now 12 years old, from the seemingly invincible new T-1000 Terminator (Robert Patrick). "I was pleased to make my Terminator into a saviour," he said, "to introduce a more sentimental side, because this allowed me to play against myself."

Both Schwarzenegger and Cameron knew that *T2* (as it became known) had to be extremely inventive to improve on the original and satisfy its discerning audience. So, where the first Terminator had been massive and unstoppable, the new Terminator was lean, mean, and remorseless in his pursuit of the young John Connor. Made of a motile metal that could assume any

> "I'd always been impressed by Arnold as a screen presence."
> **Walter Hill**

form or shape, T-1000 could imitate anything from a tiled floor to a human being. Always a director at the forefront of technology, James Cameron used the latest "morphing" effects that spiralled his budget to somewhere around $90 million (£60 million), making his "violent movie about peace" the most expensive production in Hollywood history.

Schwarzenegger was only too pleased to return to the role, and have the opportunity to demonstrate how far he had come. "Playing that role again after seven years was ideal because I'm now more equipped to play a complex character. This time the robot has to become more human, yet still has to have this dialogue like a computer spitting out information." Arnie's character, on the pretext of being a more efficient protector, tries to learn more about human behaviour, and is even introduced to street slang by John Connor, who teaches him the infamous catchphrase "Hasta la vista, baby."

T2

Filming began on October 8, 1990. Director James Cameron was as happy as his star to be back on a *Terminator* set: "I realized that *The Terminator* was the one film that I'd done that was closest to my heart and that I'd really enjoyed making just for the sheer kinetic thrill of filmmaking. So with *Terminator 2* I've now come full circle."

Cameron may have felt he had come full circle, but in fact he had come a lot further. Made for a mere $6.5 million (£4.3 million) in 1984 with a rookie director and an unproven star, *The Terminator* was a sleeper hit. Now, seven years later, Cameron was one of the biggest directors in Hollywood, Arnold was the biggest movie star in the world, and *T2* was the biggest film of the year, employing the creative talents of the very best designers and effects supervisors from such top films as *Aliens*, *Rambo*, *Predator*, *Jurassic Park*, and the team at George *Star Wars* Lucas's world-leading effects "factory" ILM.

TOTAL STARDOM

Opening in the summer of 1991, the movie took close to $40 million (£26.6 million) on its opening weekend, and went on to become the first of Arnold's movies to top the $200 million (£133 million) mark in domestic box office. The critical response for Cameron's breathtaking blend of

Saving the world: Arnold with *Terminator 2* co-stars Linda Hamilton and Joe Morton.

visionary epic, religious parable and state-of-the-art action and effects was even stronger—"As with *Aliens*, director James Cameron has again taken a first-rate science-fiction film and crafted a sequel that's in some ways more impressive—expanding on the original rather than merely remaking it," said *Variety* at the time, going on to add, "If the reported $100 million budget is a study in excess, at least a lot of it ended up on the screen." What didn't end up on the screen of course was Arnold's usual high salary, which this time was augmented with a personal Lear

The ground-breaking special effects work of *Terminator 2* was justly rewarded. *From left to right:* Linda Hamilton, James Cameron, effects maestro Stan Winston and Arnold.

TOTAL STARDOM

> "If the reported $100 million budget is a study in excess, at least a lot of it ended up on the screen."
>
> *Vanity Fair*

jet, which he had requested in lieu of a higher salary. If *T2*'s worldwide box office of over $400 million (£266 million) was anything to go by, he was worth it.

The peak of success

Now unequivocally the biggest movie star in the world, Arnold seemed to have everything: the Pentagon were even arranging his personal transportation, permitting the ex-tank driving Austrian soldier to be the first civilian to own their all-terrain vehicle, the "Humvee", widely used in the Gulf War—"I can't wait to drive up to movie premières in it."

He had succeeded in building a perfect world for himself, just as he had built the perfect body. What could possibly go wrong? What could burst Arnold Schwarzenegger's bubble?

The answer was a script called *Last Action Hero*.

***T2* proved to be the hot ticket for 1992: Arnold autographs a fan's poster.**

Last Action Hero

Following the phenomenal success of *T2*, Arnold reportedly had up to a hundred projects to choose from.

These included Paul Verhoeven's *The Crusades*, the still delayed *Sgt. Rock*, a proposed sequel to *Twins* called *Triplets* featuring Roseanne Arnold as a long-lost sister, and *Sweet Tooth*, which would see Arnold cast as the Tooth Fairy.

He opted instead for a script called *Last Action Hero* written by David Arnott and Zak Penn, the tale of a young boy with a magic ticket who enters the movie world of his screen hero Jack Slater.

Arnold saw in this the potential to combine big-budget action with all-out comedy, but right from the start the movie was an exercise in the excess of Hollywood. With a budget somewhere between $60 million and $80 million (£40 million and £53 million), with Arnie taking a percentage and $15 million (£10 million) up front, this was never going to be a cheap movie. With an intense production schedule, and the proviso that the film must be ready by the summer to capitalize on the year's busiest box-office period, the movie began to spiral out of control.

Big ticket

Hailed as the "Big Ticket for '93", *Last Action Hero* was considered by all involved to be a sure thing. Arnie executive-produced, chose the director John McTiernan, and trumpeted it at Cannes before it was even completed, giving 94 interviews in one day, a cavalier approach for which he was subsequently severely criticized by *Variety*.

The advertising was massive—60-foot inflatable Arnies astride the harbour in Cannes, a $20 million (£13.3 million) promotional tie-in with Burger King, and the first advert in space, courtesy of a rocket launch, which, let's face it, was not going to be seen by too many people. Columbia studio head Mark Canton boasted when he was still anticipating a hit: "I predict in the years to come, others will attempt to follow our aggressive distribution policy: start wide, get bigger, expand further, and never look back."

Due to the movie's extremely tight schedule, it was afforded only one test screening, which proved disastrous. Word spread through Hollywood like

Young Danny Madigan (Austin O'Brien) enters the world of his screen hero Jack Slater in the overblown *Last Action Hero* (1993).

> **"I predict in the years to come, others will attempt to follow our aggressive distribution policy: start wide, get bigger, expand further, and never look back."**
> **Mark Canton**

wildfire. "When you put yourself out there as the biggest ticket of '93," Arnold said, "you leave yourself wide open and vulnerable."

Arnold had never wanted to open his movie against Steven Spielberg's *Jurassic Park*. He admitted that "In hindsight it would have been better to postpone the opening of the movie"—and he was right. Within a few months, *Jurassic Park* had become the most financially successful movie in cinema history. *Last Action Hero* became the flop of the year, bottoming out at around a relatively minor $50 million (£33.3 million). *Premiere* magazine was succinct in its review of the film—"movie combines the action and comedy genres for the first time since… ohmigod, *Hudson Hawk*".

Post-mortem
So what went wrong? The studio blamed the press, and with reviews like "A joyless soulless machine of a movie" and "a noisy monstrosity", it is easy to see why. The impossible competition offered by *Jurassic Park* was another factor. Audiences also

LAST ACTION HERO

> "The bottom line is that this is the same press that has helped me with other movies, so you can't really complain when they choose to pick on you once in a while".
>
> **Arnold Schwarzenegger**

were confused as to what kind of a film it was: the plot said comedy, Arnold said action, and the poster had some thinking it was a kids' movie. Many people had problems with the convoluted plot, as Arnold Schwarzenegger was playing Arnold Schwarzenegger, who in turn was playing Jack Slater.

But just how bad was it? To be fair to *Last Action Hero*, somewhere among its excessive and often flat set-pieces and its brain-numbing full-volume heavy rock soundtrack there is a good film struggling to get out—McTiernan's visual flair remains undiminished, and the whole reality-versus-the-movies subplot was intriguingly more complex than expected. But overall the film will be remembered for what was wrong with it. In its own way, as with

Even the ultimate hero (*above*) was no match for *Jurassic Park* (*left*).

110

LAST ACTION HERO

so many of Arnold's movies, it remains a perfect example of its times, the ultimate Hollywood *Zeitgeist* movie for the post-Eighties—a movie that was built solely around the power of a megastar and filled with a plethora of in-jokes that relate to that star, from cameos by Sharon Stone and Robert Patrick to the overused "I'll be back" line. To add to it all, Arnie chose to play himself as Arnold the superstar, Arnold the persona. The self-referential nature of the film was inherently smug, suffused with a kind of "Here I am, aren't I as wonderful as you think I am" feeling. Such conceit is never an attractive prospect in a person, even less so in a movie.

> **"When you put yourself out there as the biggest ticket of '93, you leave yourself wide open and vulnerable."**
> **Arnold Schwarzenegger**

Last Action Hero was a reminder that things can go too far, that no one is invulnerable to failure, and that a star can get too big; and when he does, there's always one group of people who will let him know—his audience.

Characteristically, Arnold came out best from the movie, taking responsibility for his misjudgement. "First, I learned that in my case, if you don't give the people a very clear comedy or a very clear action movie, somehow the two don't mix together." Ever the diplomat, Arnold was even forgiving of the press: "The film performed poorly because the press destroyed it even before it came out...The bottom line is that this is the same press that has helped me with other movies, so you can't really complain when they choose to pick on you once in a while."

The indestructible hero?
Having reached the peak of his profession, having had it all and then seen the possibility of losing it, one thing is certain—Arnold is not going to give up without a fight. In the light of *Last Action Hero*'s failure, he is

Opposite page: Last Action Hero's explosive action and succession of in-jokes proved to be Arnold's only case of misjudging public taste.

ARNOLD SCHWARZENEGGER

Arnold in don't-notice-me celebrity shorts takes his second daughter, Christina Aurelia, for a stroll.

LAST ACTION HERO

> "I think people will be very surprised in the future by what they see me do."
>
> **Arnold Schwarzenegger**

working again with the people who best understand him, and who know how to get the best from him both as a performer and as a larger-than-life image.

His next movie will be *True Lies* for Jim Cameron, with Arnie cast as the head of an anti-nuclear terrorist government task force. After that he plans to work again with Paul Verhoeven on the long-discussed *Crusades*, and also is on the verge of green-lighting another project that reunites him with Ivan Reitman and Danny DeVito.

Arnold Schwarzenegger has reinvented himself several times in his life: bodybuilder, businessman, socialite and international movie star, first in action roles and then in comedy. He has bounced back from each defeat and defended every title he has ever won, often improving on it—so it is unlikely that he will now relinquish his claim as the movies' biggest star.

Chronology

1947
July 30 — Arnold born in Austrian town of Thal.

1962
Begins to train at the Athletic Union, Graz

1965
October 1 — National Service in Austrian army.
October 30 — Goes AWOL to enter Junior Mr Europe. Wins his first bodybuilding title.

1966
March — Wins Mr Germany title.
September — Placed second in NABBA Mr Universe contest in England.

1967
September — Becomes youngest ever Mr Universe at age of 20, in England.

1968
September — Retains Mr Universe title in England. Runner up in IFBB Mr Universe contest in America.

1969
Runner up in IFBB Mr Universe contest in America.
Retains title in NABBA Mr Universe contest in England.
Begins filming first movie *Hercules in New York* (aka *Hercules Goes Bananas*).

1970
September — Retains NABBA Mr Universe title in England.
Wins Pro Mr World title in America.
Wins Mr Olympia title.

1971
May 20 — Brother Meinhard dies in car accident.
September — Defends Mr Olympia title in Paris.

1972
September — Defends Mr Olympia title.
December — Father, Gustav, dies.

1973
Small role in Robert Altman's *The Long Goodbye*
September — Defends Mr Olympia title.

1974
Pumping Iron published.
September — Defends Mr Olympia title.

CHRONOLOGY

Appears on Lucille Ball TV special, *Happy Anniversary and Goodbye*.

1975

April	Begins filming *Stay Hungry* in Birmingham, Alabama.
November	Wins Mr Olympia for sixth time, retires on stage.
	Filmed for *Pumping Iron* movie.

1976

September	Promotes Mr Olympia contest with partner Jim Lorimer.

1977

January	Wins Golden Globe as Best Newcomer for *Stay Hungry*.
	Pumping Iron released.
	First book published, *Arnold: The Education of a Bodybuilder*.
	Attends Cannes Film Festival for first time to promote *Pumping Iron*.
August 28	Meets Maria Shriver at Robert F. Kennedy Tennis Tournament, Forest Hills.

1978

October	Films *The Villain* (aka *Cactus Jack*).

1979

May	Promotes *The Villain* at Cannes.
November	Graduates from the University of Wisconsin with a degree in business and international economics.
	Guest stars on episode of *The Streets of San Francisco*.

1980

	Co-stars in TV movie *The Jayne Mansfield Story* as former Mr Olympia Mickey Hargitay
October	Wins Mr Olympia contest for the seventh time. Contest is filmed as *The Comeback*.
	Films *Conan the Barbarian* in Spain.

1982

May	*Conan the Barbarian* released.

1983

September 9	Becomes a US citizen.
	Films *Conan the Destroyer*.

1984

	Attends Republican convention in Dallas.
March	Begins filming *The Terminator*.
July	*Conan the Destroyer* released.
September	Shooting *Red Sonja*.
November	*The Terminator* released.

1985

	Filming *Commando*
August 10	Announces engagement to Maria Shriver.

CHRONOLOGY

October	*Commando* released.
November	Buys home in Pacific Palisades; filming begins on *Raw Deal*.

1986

	Filming *Predator*
April 26	Marries Maria Shriver.
June	*Raw Deal* released.
September	Receives honorary award at Mr Olympia contest.

1987

June 2	Receives star on Hollywood Walk of Fame.
June	*Predator* released.
November	*Running Man* released.
	Receives Star of the Year Award from National Association of Theatre Owners.

1988

	Filming *Red Heat*
February	Begins shooting in Moscow.
	Filming *Twins*.
June	*Red Heat* released.
	Campaigns for Republican Presidential candidate George Bush.
December	*Twins* released.

1989

March	Filming begins on *Total Recall* in Mexico.

December	Daughter, Katherine Eunice, born to Arnold and Maria.

1990

Summer	*Total Recall* released; earns over $25 million (£16.6 million) at box office in first weekend.
October	Filming begins on *Terminator 2: Judgment Day*, which rapidly becomes the most expensive movie in Hollywood history.
December	*Kindergarten Cop* released.

1991

Summer	*T2* released; goes on to gross over $200 million (£133.3 million) in US alone.
	Second daughter, Christina Aurelia, born.

1993

	Filming *Last Action Hero*
	Promotes *Last Action Hero* at Cannes, giving 94 interviews in one day.
	Attends opening, along with Sylvester Stallone and Bruce Willis, of London's Planet Hollywood restaurant.
June	*Last Action Hero* released to bad reviews and a disappointing weekend gross of only $15 million (£10 million).
	Reunites with James Cameron to film *True Lies*.

Filmography

Hercules in New York (aka Hercules Goes Bananas)
1970 (90 mins)
Dir: Arthur A. Seidelman
Starring: Arnold Strong, Deborah Lewis, James Karen
(VPD)

The Long Goodbye
1973 (112 mins)
Dir: Robert Altman
Starring: Elliot Gould, Nina Van Pallandt, Sterling Hayden, Henry Gibson, Mark Rydell
(Warner Home Video)

Stay Hungry
1976 (102 mins)
Dir: Bob Rafelson
Starring: Jeff Bridges, Sally Field, R.G. Armstrong, Robert Englund
(Warner Home Video)

Pumping Iron
1977 (85 mins)
Dir: George Butler, Robert Fiore
Starring: Lou Ferrigno, Matty Ferrigno, Ken Waller, Franco Columbu
(Castle Hendring Video)

The Villain (aka Cactus Jack)
1979 (93 mins)
Dir: Hal Needham
Starring: Kirk Douglas, Ann-Margret, Paul Lynde, Ruth Buzzi, Jack Elam
(RCA Columbia)

The Jayne Mansfield Story
1980 (104 mins)
Dir: Dick Lowry
Starring: Loni Anderson, Ray Buktenica, Kathleen Lloyd, G.D. Spradlin
(Guild Home Video)

Conan the Barbarian
1982 (129 mins)
Dir: John Milius
Starring: James Earl Jones, Max Von Sydow, Mako, Sandahl Bergman
(Warner Home Video)

Conan the Destroyer
1984 (103 mins)
Dir: Richard Fleischer
Starring: Grace Jones, Wilt Chamberlain, Mako, Olivia D'Abo, Sarah Douglas
(RCA Columbia)

The Terminator
1984 (108 mins)
Dir: James Cameron
Starring: Michael Biehn, Linda Hamilton, Paul Winfield, Lance Henriksen
(Virgin)

Red Sonja
1985 (89 mins)
Dir: Richard Fleischer
Starring: Brigitte Nielsen, Sandahl Bergman, Paul Smith
(Cannon)

Commando
1985 (88 mins)
Dir: Mark L. Lester
Starring: Rae Dawn Chong, Dan Hedaya, Vernon Wells, David Patrick Kelly
(Fox Video)

FILMOGRAPHY

Raw Deal
1986 (106 mins)
Dir: John Irvin
Starring: Kathryn Harrold, Sam Wanamaker, Robert Davi, Ed Lauter
(Guild Home Video)

Predator
1987 (107 mins)
Dir: John McTiernan
Starring: Carl Weathers, Elpidia Carrillo, Bill Duke, Jesse Ventura
(Fox Video)

The Running Man
1987 (101 mins)
Dir: Paul Michael Glaser
Starring: Maria Conchita Alonso, Richard Dawson, Yaphet Kotto, Jesse Ventura, Jim Brown
(Braveworld)

Red Heat
1988 (103 mins)
Dir: Walter Hill
Starring: James Belushi, Peter Boyle, Ed O'Ross, Larry Fishburne
(RCA Columbia)

Twins
1988 (112 mins)
Dir: Ivan Reitman
Starring: Danny DeVito, Kelly Preston, Chloe Webb, Bonnie Bartlett
(CIC)

Total Recall
1990 (109 mins)
Dir: Paul Verhoeven
Starring: Rachel Ticotin, Sharon Stone, Ronny Cox, Michael Ironside
(Guild Home Video)

Kindergarten Cop
1990 (110 mins)
Dir: Ivan Reitman
Starring: Penelope Ann Miller, Pamela Reed, Linda Hunt, Richard Tyson
(CIC)

Terminator 2: Judgment Day
1991 (136 mins)
Dir: James Cameron
Starring: Linda Hamilton, Edward Furlong, Robert Patrick
(Guild Home Video)

Dave
1993 (110 mins)
Dir: Ivan Reitman
Starring: Kevin Kline, Sigourney Weaver, Frank Langella, Kevin Dunn, Ben Kingsley
(Warner Home Video)

Last Action Hero
1993 (130 mins)
Dir: John McTiernan
Starring: F. Murray Abraham, Charles Dance, Anthony Quinn, Austin O'Brien, Mercedes Ruehl
(Columbia TriStar)

BOOKS

Arnold: The Education of a Bodybuilder
(with Douglas Kent Hall)
Sphere Books

Arnold's Bodybuilding for Women
(with Douglas Kent Hall) Sphere Books

Arnold's Bodybuilding for Men
Sphere Books

Arnold's Encyclopedia of Modern Bodybuilding
(with Bill Dobbins)
Pelham Books

Index

Numbers in *italics* refer to pictures.

A

Altman, Robert 26
American citizenship 48, 51
Anderson, Loni 42
Ann-Margret 39
Arnold: The Education of a Body Builder 13, 37
Arnold Schwarzenegger Classic 93
Arnott, David 106
Avoriaz Film Festival award 58

B

Bachman, Richard 73, 74
Ball, Lucille 27
Belushi, James 77, 79
Bergman, Sandahl 46
Biehn, Michael 55
bodybuilding 10-35, 40-1, 42-6
Bridges, Jeff 28, 30
Bush, George 24, 25, 29, 94
Butler, George 25, 29

C

Cactus Jack (*The Villain*) 39
Cameron, James 54-6, 66, 67, 86, 100-4, 113
Cannes Film Festival 37, 40, 48, 106-7
Carney, Art 27
Chong, Rae Dawn 59, 61, 64
Collins, Joan 51
Columbu, Franco 19, 31, 71
Comeback, The 44
Commando 59-63, 64-5, 66, 67, 99
Commando 2 99
Conan the Barbarian 42, 44-8, 61
Conan the Destroyer 50-4, 58, 61
"Conan the Republican" 48-51, 94
Crusades 106, 113

D

Dave 93
Dawson, Richard 74
De Laurentiis, Dino 42, 58-9
DeVito, Danny 80-2, *80, 81*, 82, 84, *84*, 86, 113
Dick, Philip K. 86
Dobbins, Benny 78
Douglas, Kirk *8, 9*, *38*, 39
Duke and Fluffy project 100

E

Eastwood, Clint 44
engagement to Maria 62-4

F

Ferrigno, Lou 26-7, 31
Field, Sally 28
Flash Gordon 42
Fleischer, Richard 51, 53, 59
Furlong, Edward 100, 101

G

Gaines, Charles 25, 28, 29
Glaser, Paul Michael 74
Golden Globe Award 35

H

Hall, Arsenio 85
Hall, Douglas Kent 37
Hamilton, Linda *103*, 104
Happy Anniversary and Goodbye 27-8
Hercules movies 9-11
Hercules in New York 18, 19, 20-1, 22, 28
Hill, Walter 75, 76, 78, 79, 101
Hollywood Boulevard Walk of Fame, star on 74-5
Howard, Robert E. 44, 45, 59
Hurd, Gayle Anne 54

J

Jayne Mansfield Story, The 14, 42
Jones, Grace *50*, 51
Jones, Sam 42
Junior Mr Europe title 13, 19
Jurassic Park 108, *108*

K

Kennedy family 39, 48-9, 63, 71
Kindergarten Cop 51, 95-9
Kotto, Yaphet 72

INDEX

L

Last Action Hero 37, 105, 106-11
Lester, Mark 61, 62, 63
Locke, Sondra 44
Long Goodbye, The 26
Lorimer, Jim 34

M

McTiernan, John 67-8, 86, 106, 109
Marnul, Kurt 13
Milius, John 42, 44, 46-7, 51, 53
Miller, Alph 34
Morton, Joe 103
Mr America 25
Mr Olympia 19, 21, 22-5, 26-7, 35
Mr Universe 12, 14-17, 20, 22-3, 24, 31, 42-6
Mr World 22-3

N

National Association of Theatre Owner awards 58, 65, 75
National Service 13
Nielsen, Brigitte 58, 59

O

O'Bannon, Dan 86
O'Brien, Austin 107
Oliva, Sergio 19, 22
Oscar awards 26

P

Park, Reg 11, 14, 20, 22
Parton, Dolly 29
Patrick, Robert 101, 111
Penn, Zak 106
Planet Hollywood restaurants 36, 94-5, 99
Predator 51, 66-71, 73, 75, 99
Premiere Power in Hollywood list 99
President's Council on Physical Fitness and Sports 79, 92, 93
Preston, Kelly 81, 83
Pumping Iron (book and movie) 25-39, 61

R

Rafelson, Bob 28
Raw Deal 65, 66, 72-3
Reagan, Ronald 49, 51, 84, 93
Red Heat 51, 75-9
Red Sonja 58-9
Reeves, Steve 11, 11
Reitman, Ivan 80-2, 85, 93, 95, 113
The Running Man 72-5

S

Schwarzenegger, Aurelia 8, 14
Schwarzenegger, Christina 112
Schwarzenegger, Gustav 8, 25-6
Schwarzenegger, Katherine 93, 93
Schwarzenegger, Meinhard 8, 13, 23
Sgt Rock project 99, 106
Shriver, Eunice 63
Shriver, Maria 39-40, 40, 62-4, 63, 63, 66, 71, 85, 93, 93

Shusett, Ronald 86
Silver, Joel 59, 66-8
Special Olympics 63
Stallone, Sylvester 35-6, 36, 37, 58, 59, 65, 85, 93-4, 95, 99
Stay Hungry 28-9, 35, 42, 99
Steel Alan 11
Stone, Sharon 88, 111
Strong, Arnold 19, 21, 22, 29
Streets of San Francisco, The 40

T

The Terminator 20, 54-8, 61, 66, 67, 74, 99, 100
Terminator 2: Judgment Day 57, 100-5
Total Recall 85-92, 99
True Lies 113
Twins 51, 80-5, 86, 99
Tyson, Mike 82

V

Van Damme, Jean Claude 65, 66
Verhoeven, Paul 86, 88, 91-2, 106, 113
The Villain (Cactus Jack) 39, 48

W

Waldheim, Kurt 71
Wayne, John 9, 9, 68
wedding 66, 70-1
Weider, Joe 15, 17-20, 22
Willis, Bruce 94, 95, 99
Winston, Stan 104
Wisconsin University degree 40